unfortunate english

unfortunate english

The Gloomy Truth
Behind the Words You Use

Bill Brohaugh

WRITER'S DIGEST BOOKS

writersdigestbooks.com
Cincinnati, Ohio

Distributed in Canada by Fraser Direct, 100 Armstrong Avenue, Georgetown, ON, Canada L7G 5S4, Tel: (905) 877-4411. Distributed in the U.K. and Europe by David & Charles, Brunel House, Newton Abbot, Devon, TQ12 4PU, England, Tel: (+44) 1626 323200, Fax: (+44) 1626 323319, E-mail: mail@davidandcharles. co.uk. Distributed in Australia by Capricorn Link, P.O. Box 704, Windsor, NSW 2756 Australia, Tel: (02) 4577-3555.

Visit our Web site at www.writersdigest.com for information on more resources for writers.

To receive a free weekly e-mail newsletter delivering tips and updates about writing and about Writer's Digest products, register directly at our Web site at http://newsletters.fwpublications.com.

10 09 08 07 06   5 4 3 2 1

Library of Congress Cataloging-in-Publication Data

Brohaugh, William.

 Unfortunate English: the gloomy truth behind the words you use / by Bill Brohaugh. -- 1st ed.

     p. cm.

 Includes bibliographical references and index.

 ISBN 13: 978-1-58297-443-9
 ISBN 10: 1-58297-443-8 (hardcover : alk. paper)

 1. English language--Etymology. 2. English language--Terms and phrases. 3. English language--History. I. Title.

 PE1574.B64 2006

 422--dc22   2006018710

Edited by Jane Friedman
Designed by Claudean Wheeler
Illustrations by J. Cobb / Instreme Interactive
Production coordinated by Robin Richie

dedication

I dedicate this book to Dennis Chaptman, who has been as long as I've known him my articulate and creative friend, and the holder of the missing piece of my persona. Give it back, dammit.

taBLe of coNteNts

introduction

One morning, while browsing John Ayto's *Dictionary of Word Origins: The Histories of More Than 8,000 English-Language Words*, I came upon this entry:

hoi polloi *see polyp*

Hoi polloi? Polyp? Was this some sort of elitist commentary, equating the general masses with a potentially cancerous growth? (I didn't really think that, but it does make for some interesting musing.)

Turns out that the syllable common to *hoi polloi* and *polyp*—*pol*—traces back to the Greek root *pollus*, "many." *Polyp* originally denoted an octopus (a "many-footed" creature), and the word was metaphorically applied to the tentacled growth we now know as a polyp. *Hoi polloi*? Literal Greek, meaning "the many."

In the parlance, Whoda thunk it?

Such are the wondrous discoveries awaiting us when we examine word histories. Unseen connections (as in *hoi polloi* and *polyp*) and unseemly associations, as well (as we'll see throughout this book).

Deep within the histories of many words, you'll find secrets and surprises and origins that might chafe the sensitive: You'll find bodily functions in words like *fizzle* and *poppycock*, war and mayhem in words like *belfry* and *ovation*, drunkenness in words like *bridal* and *symposium*, insults in words like *pretty* and *coax*, medieval torture in words like *travel* and *guy*, unpleasant thoughts for the squeamish in words like *muscle* and *porcelain*.

You'll find, as the saying almost goes, skeletons in the verbal closets. (That phrase, by the way, did *not* arise the way the popular Internet etymology would have it: that ancient doctors proudly hid the skeletons formerly owned by the cadavers they dissected in their studies. Some keepsake, that.) *Unfortunate English* opens the closet. The pages that follow alert you to the improprieties, disgusting notions, licentiousness, and other foul thoughts that you speak daily without realizing it. I'll point out what sensibilities you'd be offending if people took the words you use for their original meanings.

This book concentrates on words that—at their core—had meanings or origins less than savory to today's thinking, to today's word usage. It pays very little attention to words that may have taken a pejorative or unseemly meaning along the way. These words simply got dressed up in different clothing as time went on, donning a metaphorical mask or a euphemistic costume or a slang-conversion disguise. For example, *aunt* always meant sister of one of your parents. For a time, it was used as a euphemism for mistress or whore. *Aunt* is therefore not originally an unseemly word, and therefore not covered in this book. On the other hand, *spill* had bloody meanings from the very beginning, until the word softened to the quietly sloppy word it is today. And thus, *spill* gets its due here. Occasionally, I dip back into what the word meant in the language it was borrowed from, even though its original use in English was innocuous and straightforward. For instance, *lasagna* in English has always meant the Italian multilayered pasta dish. But the Latin word that led to *lasagna* arises from … well, you don't want to know (but I'll tell you anyway in the chapter called "And This Is What We Put *Into* Our Mouths?").

Keep in mind, too, that the origins discussed here might not be offensive in and of themselves, but they are presented here because they might be out of joint with modern sensibilities and some political or social movements or agendas. For instance, I have no problem with enjoying a few drinks—neither the concept nor the actual performance. I'll likely pop a beer myself after completing my writing day's work.

3

But alcohol watchdogs might be taken aback at the words that resulted from association with drink.

Some words, of course, have meanings out of joint with almost everyone's sense of propriety, whether words of torture, violent bloodletting, smelly bodily functions, or blush-blush body parts boldly displayed in public.

Finally, this book does not pretend to be any sort of comprehensive language history or explication of the many mechanisms of word creation and how words change in meanings, spellings, and uses. I've listed several excellent sources for such investigations; many exacting and intelligent people have devoted themselves to the intricacies of etymology, and they've shared their expertise and their findings in reference books both scholarly and popular. *Unfortunate English* shares curmudgeonly smartass observations about individual histories and theories of histories; this book is simply rounding up the unusual suspects and explaining how they secreted themselves into their current meanings. (And if the use of the word *smartass* in the previous sentence bothers you, gird yourself.)

At least we can take comfort that these polyps—these disgusting precancerous growths—are largely today benign.

them's fightin' words!

words of war and the battlefield

The words discussed in this chapter are, in a sense, wolves in sheep's uniform. They wear the guise of innocent everyday speech, with the attire of war underneath.

And we've just passed by the first example of such a word, most of us barely noting it as it hides, camouflaged, on that ancient battlefield. The phrase "attire of war" in the paragraph above is redundant—in the original sense of the word attire. Attire by the mid-1200s originally meant "accoutrements of war, for man or for warhorse."

Around the year 1300 it was being used in the more general sense.

The disguises donned by the words of war can be quite pretty (in that pretty originally meant "artful or cunning"—see the listing for PRETTY for details). For example, petticoat very early on was a word of the battlefield. A petticoat was originally a small coat worn by men, part of the layering of fifteenth-century garb. But early in its history, a petticoat was also a padded garment that provided additional protection beneath armor. And that armor and petticoat could make the soldiers look pretty (in that pretty for a time was used to describe fine and handsome men—including stout, warlike, and ready-for-battle men).

On the pages that follow, then, words of war, weaponry, the battlefield, and the military. We hear echoes of gunshots and warriors' cries in everything from a day of the week to a letter of the alphabet. We begin by sounding the alarm.

aLarm

In an etymologically perfect world, no pacifists would have alarm clocks.

It's not that they need the extra sleep (and besides, snooze buttons take care of that concern).

Nor would pacifists have smoke alarms, or respond to fire alarms.

The pacifists might be surprised but certainly not alarmed to discover what that little beeping clock or the whining smoke detector or the shrieking fire siren are, in a sense, really shouting to them: "To arms! To arms!"

The first use of *alarm* was as a rally cry. "To the weapons!" shouted the rallying defenders, who, because they were Italian, actually shouted "*All' arme!*" The French borrowed the shout into Old French as "*Alarme!*" and by the late 1300s, threatened English speakers were also shouting thusly. Soon after the interjection came to English, it found its role as a noun describing the shout itself. By the mid- to late 1500s, the more general senses of both warning and warning device had come to *alarm*.

If nonviolent sorts choose not to be alarmed by this word's origin, perhaps they can instead be *afraid* in the original sense of the word. To *affray* people was to disturb them, alarm them. These people were *affrayed*, which we now use with different spelling and different meaning as *afraid*.

So, the original alarm was sounded as a rally to take weapon and make war; it was a battle cry. An alert to medieval threat. Which is why when my alarm clock goes off I hack it to pieces with a halberd.

sLogan

Ever feel besieged by slogans? Even the old ones ring in our ears, having battered us so much. "You deserve a break today" and "Lucky Strike Means Fine Tobacco" and "Where's the beef?"

The slogans ring in our ears like the cries of blood-lusting warriors. Which is what the original slogans were. Sixteenth-century Scottish Highlanders and Irishmen shouting a place or a name associated with them (think "Wallace! Wallace!" in the movie *Braveheart*) before rushing in to skewer your skull not with facile words but with mauling, decapitating weapons. Or similar shouting during the battle to identify fellow clansmen. A *slogorne* could also be a watchword.

By the early 1700s, the meaning had softened to mean any phrase that was distinctive and specific to a person or entity (in essence, synonymous with *motto*) and by the 1900s had come to its meaning of a catchphrase. (I picture legions of doughboys—Poppin' Fresh Doughboys—giggling maniacally, storming a determined phalanx of Scrubbing Bubbles and screeching, "Nothing says lovin' like something from the oven!")

In sports, some team cheers might be considered akin to the original *slogornes*. In many ways, the bloodlust remains.

BeLfry

As crazy as it may sound, there were almost certainly no bats in the original belfry. And most likely no bells.

Though the meaning of "bell tower" was also early in the word's history, the original belfry, back in Middle English, was an instrument of war. A belfry was a movable siege tower. In fact, the word was later applied to watchtowers (with alarm bells, presumably), and then to the bell room in church towers and steeples.

The first syllable was originally *ber-* and not *bel-*, but in a consonant shift, people began using *belfry*. The change had nothing to do specifically with bells, other than the fact that the similarity of *bel-* to *bell* encouraged people to think of the word in its current meaning. (Shifting between *R*s and *L*s occurs because of the smaller position of the tongue used to pronounce each sound.) This partnership helped *bel-* and *bell* win out in both spelling and meaning. And thusly, the church tower defeated the siege tower, likely all because of a single letter.

Which letter?

The *L*, you say?

Shh. You shouldn't say *L* in church.

bicker, cope

Bickering connotes almost a lifestyle shared by two people, a way they relate to each other. To *bicker* is "to quarrel or disagree constantly."

And when you see a couple bickering, you rarely worry that the verbal sparring will come to blows.

Odd, since bickering came *from* blows.

To *bicker* by the 1300s was "to fight physically, to exchange blows." The figurative sense of "quarrel" came by the mid-1400s. In the 1400s, the word had a now-obsolete meaning of "to exchange volleys of arrows or slingshot." It's odd to think of the archers of two warring armies bickering, but bicker they did, with deadly force.

Bickering is a way of coping with each other—in the sense that to *cope* originally meant, yes, "to come to blows." In Late Middle English, to *cope* with an enemy was "to battle" with that enemy, to meet in combat or contest. There was no original sense of outcome as there is in the word today. By the late 1500s, *cope* meant "to battle well, to prove yourself a worthy opponent." Again, no sense of outcome. By the mid-1600s, the modern sense of figurative contention had arrived and had begun to imply success in the coping. Bickering is now not a good thing, though better than it was. Coping, on the other hand, is a good thing indeed.

But in the original senses of these words, as Muhammad Ali did not say, "Cope like a butterfly, bicker like a bee."

medLey

And now, a medley of War's greatest hits . . .

Pow! Slash! Thwack!

What, you were expecting clips from oldies band War (with or without Eric Burdon)? Songs like "Low Rider" or "The Cisco Kid" or "Why Can't We Be Friends?"

Well, especially not "Why Can't We Be Friends?" because the War being discussed here is combat.

The medley we hear—*pow! slash! thwack!*—is the sound of one army battling another in hand-to-hand combat, what we term "melee combat."

In fact, the words *medley* and *melee* are closely related, arising from Old French words meaning "a mixture." When *medley* came to English by the early 1300s, it meant mixing in battle, hoards of warriors swarming and killing. Gentler figurative meanings of "mixture" followed shortly.

But in its earliest sense, *medley* was what we slangishly refer to as "mixing it up," and the greatest hits were deadly ones.

caddie

A caddie helps you shoot a round of golf.

In the earliest sense of the word, had he the weaponry at the time, he'd likely be shooting a few rounds himself. With guns.

A *caddie* is a diminutive word deriving from *cadet*, a type of military serviceman. By the early 1700s, a caddie was a general helper. By the mid 1800s, the caddie was the toter of a different type of arsenal, golf clubs (which are not military-type weapons, though the occasional tree attacked in golfing frustration might disagree).

tuesday

Scheduling note for antiwar demonstrators: Best not schedule any protests for Tuesday.

Tuesday is named for the Norse god of war, Tyr (known as Tiw by the Anglo-Saxons).

Tuesday's a good day for gods of war, it seems. In French, Tuesday is *mardi* (as in Mardi Gras, "Fat Tuesday"). Mardi is named after Mars, the Roman god of war. (This is not a coincidence. When the Anglo-Saxons adopted the Roman seven-day week, they used the names of their gods that corresponded with the Roman gods, and Tiw was the Anglo-Saxon equivalent of Mars. French retained the Roman reference in its names of days of the week.)

And as long as we're scheduling, best take some time off in March, as well. A whole month of Mars-days.

host

A large number of any given thing is a host: a host of good ideas, a host of selections at the smorgasbord, a host of hosts at the Hotel and Restaurant Professionals convention.

That host of foods at the buffet is probably big enough to feed an army—big enough to feed a *host*.

Before its figurative use arose by the early 1600s, a host ("big group," not "opposite of *guest*") was an imposingly large number of armed men. Better hope that buffet is indeed big enough to feed an army, lest they get *hostile*—a word ultimately from the same Latin root as the armed *host*.

Loophole

A loophole is an opening, an escape clause in the negative—the clause that doesn't exist and presents a way out. As you can quickly imagine, the first loopholes were physical holes. Openings in walls. But they weren't means of escape, unless you considered the release of arrows as "escape."

Loopholes were vertical holes in the walls of fortifications. The outer part of the hole was small, and a poor target for attackers. This narrow hole widened to allow room for movement by the archer, who would loose arrows at attackers. Early loopholes, therefore, did not involve legal battles, but physical ones.

Sally

Often expressed as "sally forth" (what ho! off we go!), to *sally* means "to rush forward" or "to embark." For example, "Let's sally forth on our Florida vacation!"

There's an irony in that vacation plan. Heading off to a vacation spot after being besieged by the hassles and stresses of the workaday world. Bursting out to retake sanity.

The original meaning of *sally* is something like that. To *sally* is to suddenly counterattack a besieging army by rushing forth from a defensive position. It is a word of war, the noun and the verb borrowed from French at the same time by the mid-1500s. (A 1542 reference uses *sally* to mean the defensive position from which the responding attack originates.) The sense of to engage in a less militaristic sortie was in use by the late 1500s.

What is perhaps not salient or noticeable in this discussion is *sally*'s relationship to other words of war: *assault*, *assail*, and *salient*. All these words reach back to Latin *salire*, "to jump, leap." (*Sauté*—probably from fats leaping about the pan—traces back to this word, too.) *Salient* as an adjective, in use by the late 1700s, means "prominent, conspicuous." *Salient* as a noun, in use by the early 1800s, was a protruding military position or a part of a military fortification.

jostLe

Ever jostle for position? Trying to get in line to get quickly selling tickets? Or to maneuver for a prime seat at a concert? Or to land dibs on the last latte at the coffee shop? You don't always win, do you?

Probably your lance isn't pointy enough.

Jostle originally was spelled *justle*, and was a form of *joust*—as in the fellows on horseback engaging in sport/combat.

For a time around 1400, *justle* also meant "to engage in sex," though the meaning wasn't widespread and of course is now out of use. That's too bad, as there could have been some good pointy-lance jokes availed by the word (which, considering the origins of slang in general, is probably why the word took the sexual meaning in the first place).

aRRaNGe

Tips for home flower arranging:

1. Protect the flanks. The enemy will seek to outmaneuver you and cave in the ends of your floral battle lines.
2. Protect your supply lines. A crafty enemy will seek to isolate your flowers from their vital resources and reinforcements.

3. Use your most destructive flowers in the central lines. Snapdragons and gladioli will do. Garlic, though not floral, will make for good reinforcements.

Pretty serious stuff, this arranging.

After all, *arrange* began with a purely military sense. You arranged your troops (the *ranks*—which is a related word) and your battle lines, and nothing else. When *arrange* reached more common use by the early 1800s, it had taken its present, more general meaning. So mount those snapdragons! Prepare to brandish your gladioli! Garlic at the ready!

Now, for those valiant floral defenders you have arranged: The origin of *snapdragon*, of course, is apparent right there in the word itself. The flowers of snapdragons resemble the heads of the mythical creatures, and if you squeeze one, the dragon's "mouth" opens. The meaning of *gladiolus* is not nearly as obvious, though also based on resemblance. This flower is named after a weapon: the sword. *Gladiolus* "stems" from the Latin *gladius*, also the root of *gladiator*. The gladiolus is so named because of its sword-shaped leaves and literally means "little sword." *Garlic* has similar etymological origins. *Gar* from Old English means "spear," and garlic is the "spear-leek," likely because of the clove's resemblance to a spearhead.

As Shakespeare thankfully did not say, a gladiolus by any other name would cut as deep.

tROpHY

After routing an enemy, the Greeks would build a monument to the victory, hanging armor and weapons and other loot taken from the enemy in public view—originally on the battlefield itself. This was a *tropaion*, and is the source of our word *trophy* (through Latin and then French). The tropaion was then dedicated to one of the Greek gods.

Trophy had taken its modern meaning by the mid-1500s (first recorded in 1569 in a work by Edmund Spenser).

Battery

They keep going and going and going, those batteries in the old TV commercials.

So do the artillery batteries in more or less constant wars through human history.

The words are related by a bit of analogic poetry. Batteries—artillery—discharge ordnance. Batteries—electrical cells—discharge electricity. Simple as that. (Artillery became known as *battery* because of what it did to its targets. It battered them, delivering battering or *battery* in the original sense of the word that survives in the phrase "assault and battery." People who undergo batteries of medical tests can understand this underlying sense as well. People besieged by a battery of drumming bunnies can, too.)

Oddly enough, an obsolete meaning of *battery* is specifically "beating drums," perhaps as a signal to charge into battle. So next time you pop some dry cells into that drumming bunny that keeps going and going and going, be sure to yell "Incoming!" first.

first-string, second-string, etc.

How poetic if the concept of first-string players on a team (the best, most prominent, and most frequently used) came from the symphony—perhaps on the analogy of the first violin being the premiere violinist, and so on.

But the strings are not musical. They are military. The first string is the bowstring in use by an archer. Second string is the backup.

Related, if someone is wound up a little too tight, we refer to them as "high-strung." And, yes, archery is the source.

fLasH iN tHe paN

Pacifism as a movement is certainly not a flash in the pan—one bright spark and little effect. But a flash in the pan is something of unintentional pacifism, a frustrated violent action.

Flintlock muskets—weapons of violence, those—relied on sparking gunpowder in a pan to set off the gun's charge. If the primer flashed but failed to ignite the shot, nothing happened—thus the source of the figurative phrase.

bLockBuster

At the extremes in the entertainment world, a book or a movie can be a fabulously successful blockbuster or a dismally performing bomb.

In the figurative sense, a bomb is obviously not a blockbuster.

In the literal sense, a bomb can be a blockbuster. And a blockbuster is definitely a bomb.

Blockbuster bombs were used by the Royal Air Force (RAF) in World War II (newspapers, not the RAF, invented and popularized the term). Indeed the bombs were designed to be powerful enough to blow up a block—in the British sense of "large building" rather than the American sense of "city block." One goal was to blow the roofs off the buildings so the incendiaries could reach inside. The bombs weighed several tons. The first, weighing two tons, was dropped over Emden, Germany, in April 1941.

So, next time you crack the spine of the latest blockbuster novel, imagine death raining from the sky (which actually would describe the plots of a number of bestsellers over the years).

ovation

When you give someone an ovation, you are in the original sense of the word celebrating that person's mediocrity. Hey! You did good, though your performance was a little so-so! Nice try! Better luck next time!

Receiving an ovation was, from ancient Roman history, an acknowledgment of second best, short of triumph. A triumph was originally a grand celebration honoring the return of a victorious Roman army and its commander. It lasted the day, and involved a grand processional in which the commander rode in a gilded chariot and would be preceded by prisoners of war (the more important, the better). During this celebration, the commander would receive laurels—literal ones in a laurel crown.

An ovation, on the other hand, was a more subdued processional honoring the return of commanders of less success. They didn't completely win the battle. Or they didn't kill enough enemies. Or the enemies were too low on the scale of Enemy Importance (such as winning a battle with pirates). They fell short of "triumphal" return into Rome. An ovation was indeed praise, yet no chariots for these guys; they had to walk (insert "standing ovation" joke here). Later on, at least they got to ride in on horseback. No laurel crown; they got myrtle. No trumpet fanfare.

By the mid-1600s, *ovation* came to mean a figurative exultation, and by the mid-1800s, it was used to describe the show of approval, applause, and the like.

But in etymological terms, giving someone an ovation has two underlying insults:

1. Hey, you were good … at killing people.
2. But, though we appreciate the effort and will let you know that, you weren't good enough.

23

weLL-HeeLeð

If you are well-heeled, you have enough money to cope with just about any situation. By being heeled, you are figuratively armed (and, ultimately, figuratively heeled, as well).

So goes a common explanation (one that has not been absolutely documented but has not been seriously disputed, either). In the American West, a frontiersman was well-heeled (or just heeled) if he carried a gun.

This, it is said, is an extension of a cockfighting term from the 1800s: Well-heeled gamecocks had spurs (natural or artificially attached) large enough to allow them to fight well.

Myself (and this is pure musing), I wonder if the fact that the end of a rifle stock is called a *heel* had some factor in the meaning of heeled as "armed."

Either way, it's likely that being well-heeled and able to fight monetarily rose from the ability to fight physically. Doc Holliday has been quoted as saying to Ike Clanton before the gunfight at the O.K. Corral, "Heel yourself and stay that way." Ike Clanton did *not* respond to the good Doc, "Physician, heel thyself."

upshot

What was the upshot of the situation? Was it what you were aiming for?

The word *upshot*, in use by the early 1500s, is not rooted in battle, though it is rooted in battle skill. The upshot was the final shot in a round of an archery contest. The word took figurative use (synonymous with the idiom "parting shot") and by the late 1500s was used to mean "conclusion or completion." This extended to mean "result," as in the common modern sense of the word, by the early 1800s.

The upshot, by the way, was taken at a target—and battle implications are at play here, too. The first use of the word *target* was as a type of shield or buckler. You didn't want to aim for the shields in battle, but you did want to aim for them when they were used for practicing your archery skills. So the sense changed from "a shield to be aimed at" to anything to be aimed at in general.

Z

Beware the wizard. He carries a concealed weapon.

It is the letter Z, concealed right there in the middle of the word *wizard*.

Our modern alphabet traces back through Latin and Etruscan and Greek to Phoenician. Phoenician letters symbolized some everyday concepts, such as ox, house, water, and fence (*aleph*, *beth*, *mem*, and *heth*—ancestors of *A*, *B*, *M*, and *H*, respectively).

All well and good, until we get to *zayin*, the ancestor of Z. The letter *zayin* symbolizes "weapon" or "sword." Object of mayhem. Ironically, the Phoenician letter *zayin* more closely resembles the letter *I* than it does our modern-day Z. It is as if the letter toppled forward a bit over the centuries, like a stick figure dying—perhaps stabbed in the back with a weapon.

Take another look at Z now. Three slashes, a weapon brandished. Whoosh whoosh whoosh. The legend of Zorro.

It is the final stroke.

it pains me to say

words of assault, torture, bloodletting, and death

We all know of sticks and stones and breaking bones and words that will never harm you. With that cliché firmly in mind, we look into some words that nowadays intend no harm, yet we find a good lot of sticks and stones in their origins, and painful pointy things as well. Many of the words today have their history in violence, torture, and pain … and now, one might say, these words fall upon death ears.

You'll find the examination of these words thrilling … and not in a good way.

thRiLL

You know the phrase, "a thrill a minute." That could be good, could be bad, depending on what kind of thrill you end up with. The good thrills are beneficial or benign. In fact, I can see thrill on your face at this moment. Two of them, actually. Yup, plain as the nose on your face: Nostrils. Nose-thrills, ultimately.

The bad thrills? Well, being thrilled by a sword or a lance was not a good thing.

A *thrill* in its earliest meaning was a hole (thus *nostrils*—"nose holes"). The verb *thrill* was "to pierce or create a hole." To bore or penetrate or drill. As one might do with a sword, and indeed the word *thrill* was used frequently in the context of such pointy weapons as the aforementioned swords and lances. So you wouldn't be particularly thrilled with the idea of being thrilled.

Shakespeare used the figurative sense of *thrill* the verb, with the idea of piercing or penetrating someone with emotion or excitement. Hopefully leaving no holes.

spLit

"Our relationship is on the rocks. It was all pretty stormy anyway. So we split."

Figurative shipwreck, that. Unknowingly appropriate, in that the word *split*, when adapted from Middle Dutch by the late 1500s, was used in the context of storms and rocks tearing ships apart, though general uses were perhaps just moments behind.

sarcasm

We're more right than we realize when we say that a sarcastic soul can rip someone to shreds with sarcastic repartee. Those shreds may now be figurative, but in the Late Greek word on which *sarcasm* is based, those shreds were quite literal.

The *sarc* in *sarcasm* comes from *sark* or *sarx*, meaning "flesh" in the Greek (thus *sarcophagus*—a coffin encasing flesh), and the Greek verb *sarkazein* meant "to tear flesh like dogs." That meaning was already producing weakened and figurative variations, with senses like "to gnash teeth" and "to speak bitterly," before it was adapted into Late Latin and then into English by the mid-1550s with the figurative sense that has, fortunately, less bite than it originally had.

iconoclast

You know the iconoclast. Violent fellow. Smashing things, destroying art and statues, inciting riots, and …

But wait a moment, you say. Iconoclasts might try to tear down some traditional notions. They assail dogma and long-standing institutions. They run against the grain, but they aren't tearing apart the wood when they do it. They may at their worst run riot, but they wouldn't inspire one.

In today's figurative sense of the word *iconoclast* (from the mid-1800s), all that is true. But the original iconoclasts destroyed things of great beauty. Think of when the Taliban took control of Afghanistan. They destroyed priceless works of art, including a fifty-three-meter statue of Buddha carved into a cliff face in Bamiyan, Afghanistan. The Taliban hated these religious artworks as false gods, as idols, as icons. In destroying these idols, the Taliban were icon-breakers. And that's what *iconoclast* means in its Greek origins.

The first iconoclasts were Christians in the eighth and ninth centuries who fought idolatry by banning the display of religious images or destroyed them outright (in raging mobs, by one description). The word surfaced in English when applied to similar destruction of Catholic religious artwork and other religious symbols and objects during the Protestant Reformation. And not just artwork was destroyed during Reformation iconoclasm. Iconoclasm spurred riots;

lives were lost. The original meaning of *iconoclasm* has been lost, but sadly the fervor that inspired the word—as evidenced by the deadly 2005 riots over Danish cartoons of Mohammed—has not.

The imagery destroyed by the iconoclast is now figurative. It was once quite literal. And often quite vicious.

HAGGLE

Bargain hunters are often skilled at haggling. They're able to slash prices, hacking away at them a bit clumsily and with sharp instruments.

Haggling originally involved physical slashing and hacking. To *haggle* was "to mangle or mutilate with sharp instruments, to chop or cut repeatedly or raggedly." These are the skills that serve different sorts of hunters, perhaps, but if I were a shopkeeper and someone were coming at me with sharp things, I suspect I'd be prone to drop the prices of my wares *before* the haggling began.

TRAVEL

Oh, the travails of travel. Long lines at airport checkpoints, missed connections, lost baggage, being tormented with ancient instruments of torture . . .

One such torture instrument was the *trepalium*, which employed three stakes (or pales)—the word was formed in Latin from *tria* ("three") and *palus* ("stake"). The precise mechanism of the instrument is not certain, which we're probably thankful for, but it's been said that fire was involved. Old French adopted the assumed Latin word *tripaliare* ("to torture") as *travailler*, which meant "to trouble" in addition to "to torture," and which eventually came to mean "to work hard or labor." *Travail*, in Old French, was pretty much what we know the word to be today—"tribulation, trouble, pain, or anguish."

When *travail* as a verb was taken into English (from the verb *travailler*, to be technical), it meant "to torment, trouble, labor, be afflicted."

So how does *travel* fit in with *trepalium*?

More pertinent is, how does *travel* fit in with *travail*?

They're the same word.

With a different syllabic emphasis and a specialized spelling, *travel* came to mean "journey"—because travel in the Middle Ages had its troubles and its tortures (lacking stakes) and its travails.

Side note: The labor within the meanings of the noun *travail* could be the labor of a worker, or the labor of a woman giving birth, a certain torture, that (I'm told).

CRISSCROSS

In your travels, you might crisscross the country, going from here to there to there to here again. And the word *crisscross* ultimately results—as did the word *travel*—from literally tortuous origins. Despite what it sounds like, *crisscross* is not an alteration of the word *cross*, a playful reduplication of a syllable, using the word-creation method that resulted in *dillydally* and *flimflam*. *Crisscross* is a spelling variant of "Christ cross," the central symbol of Christianity, based on another sort of torture—crucifixion.

The word arose in the 1400s to describe a cross-like symbol placed at the beginning of hornbooks that featured such documents as the alphabet and the Lord's Prayer. The pronunciation of *Christcross* followed the same pattern as "Christ mass" becoming the *crissmiss*-pronounced *Christmas*. A spelling change to *crisscross* followed the pronunciation, and figurative uses of the word begin *their* travels by the early 1800s as a verb (and late 1800s as a noun).

By the mid-1600s, *crisscross* as a noun was used as a synonym for *alphabet*.

CRANK

There are any number of things that can make a person cranky. Getting up on the wrong side of the bed. Getting stuck in rush-hour traffic. Being felled on the battlefield.

The crank—the tool used to rotate something, such as when trying to start an engine in the early days of the automobile—comes from Old English *crancstaef*, a reel used in weaving. *Cranc* apparently traces back to a verb meaning "to fall in battle," from the image of the wounded soldier curling himself up, taking bent form.

Being cranky once meant being ill or sick (the German word for "ill" is *krank*), and now, with the idea of having a twisted or crooked temperament, grouchy.

And if the thought of a human lying on the battlefield and curled up in agony and probably dying makes you cringe . . . *cringe* traces back to the same source as *crank*.

DERRICK

Imagine this fictitious TV game show scene:

"Vanna, are there any *D*s on the board? *D* as in *death*."

Vanna turns one letter, the first letter of a single seven-letter word.

D as in *death*.

D as in *derrick*. Or, more appropriately, *Derick*.

In sixteenth-century England, Derick was an executioner. He was accomplished in the general art of execution, including beheading. But he was especially known for his skill as a hangman. So infamous was he that his very name became associated with the grisly craft (in much the way that Mr. Boycott lent his name to a type of protest and the way that Ms. Bloomer lent her name to a type of garment). A hangman could be called a derrick, a hanging could be called a derrick, and the gallows itself could be called a derrick.

A bit of poetry was later applied to hoisting machinery that resembled gallows, and the word was eventually extended to mean other tall structures, primarily the derrick of an oil rig.

So, Vanna then fictitiously turns the rest of the letters of the seven-letter word that begins with *D* as in *death*. *Derrick*.

And why have we invited Vanna into this scenario? *Wheel of Fortune* is a glitzed TV version of a children's word-guessing game. Guess the letters of a word that your opponent selects, one by one. Fill in the letter if you guess right. Add a line to a stick figure if you are wrong. The game ends when you either guess the word or complete the stick figure, who is hanging at the end of a noose in the game called "Hangman."

bask

Imagine a theatrical trailer for an upcoming horror flick: *Bask in the Sun*.

Pretty lame name for a horror flick, you'd be thinking.

Until you realize that *bask* originally meant "to bathe or wallow in warm liquid" and was often associated with immersion in blood. From John Gower's *Confessio Amantis* (1393): "The child lay bathend in her blood . . . And for the blood was hote and warme He basketh him about therinne." So when you bask in the sunshine, you're basking in light as warm as blood itself. In fact, it is that image—of sucking up some sunshine—that brought the figurative meaning to *bask*. Shakespeare, in *As You Like It*, wrote: "As I do live by food, I met a fool/Who laid him down and bask'd him in the sun...."

Another original meaning of *bask* was "to bathe in warm water," but taking a warm bath is pretty lame for a horror movie, too. That's why *Psycho* has a shower scene.

SWING

No playground is complete without a swing.

Nor, swing-less, is a battleground complete. Nor, for that matter, any field of violence.

Playgrounds are not fields of violence, of course— or aren't supposed to be, despite little Johnny hauling off and whacking little Freddy on the back with a plastic truck. But little Johnny's aggression is far more in line with the original meaning of *swing* than that bit of playground equipment with the seats at the ends of heavy-duty chain.

To *swing* back in the days when Old English was spoken was "to flog (as in with whips), to beat, or to strike with a weapon." One sense of *swing* was "to beat the blood out of someone."

By the mid-1300s, *swing* could mean "to attempt to hit someone with a weapon, and by the early 1400s, *swing* could mean "to brandish a weapon," waving it to and fro, and the to-and-fro aspect of such swinging led by the mid-1500s to the pendulous connotation inherent in most of our modern uses of this word.

The sense of flogging or striking did *not* lead to the slang use of *swing* for another type of punishment and violence—as in *swing*, meaning "to be hanged." Though there are unintentional echoes in the slang use, to *swing* was simply an extension of "to swing from the end of a rope," that rope being a noose.

An early softening of the violent verb to *swing* entered into cookery in Old English and stuck around for a while, such as in this recipe instruction for pudding (see also PUDDING) from the 1400s: "Take the blode and swyng hit with thy hand and cast a way the lumpys that kyeneth," or "Take the blood and hand-beat it, and cast away the lumps that form." To *swing* in this sense is "to beat," as we do in modern kitchens to eggs and cream and such. Beat those eggs! Flog them! In the case of the medieval recipe quoted here, it was blood being beaten in preparing blood pudding.

In the original sense of swing, the blood being beaten was human.

ðreary

Once upon a midnight gory,
While I pondered 'bout this story …

In Old English, *dreor* was flowing blood. (*Dreor* arises from a root meaning "flow" or "fall"; *dreor* was a specific type of flow—that of blood.)

Bloody stuff is usually pretty horrid, and bloody people are in dire straits, and *dreary* came to mean "horrid" or "dire." People in bloodied states are usually not happy about it, and early on *dreary* also meant "frightened" or "sad." By the mid-1600s—more likely a softening of "dire or horrid" rather than a twist on "frightened or sad"—the word was applied to situations that make you sad: gloomy, dreary conditions.

So the tales of Poe were not only dreary, they were dreary.

BONfiRE

Crisp autumn night. Celebrate winning an election. Commemorate the defeat of a plot to blow up the Houses of Parliament (November 5 is Bonfire Night in England—see also GUY). Rally some pep for an upcoming football game. Toast some marshmallows. Burn some heretics. Torch some bones.

All have been done in a bonfire. A bonefire.

Don't be deceived by the *E* missing from modern spelling. The first syllable has nothing to do with the French word for "good"—*bon*. A bonfire was originally the burning of bones—not always as grisly as you might expect, in the case of burning refuse. But in the case of burning human beings, pretty damn grisly. The word eventually came to mean any large outdoor pyre.

As an aside, this note from the Edenbridge Bonfire Society Web site (from England, talking about the November 5 celebration): "One of the best parts of Bonfire Night is bonfire food. Try baking potatoes in the bonfire, sausages cooked over the flames, and marshmallows toasted in the fire. Of course, ask an adult to help you—fire can be dangerous." Just ask the heretics.

Ðrat!

"Curses! Foiled again." So goes the cliché exclamation of the frustrated melodrama villain. "Drat it!" he might say. Or in a fit of even more vicious mild cursing, "Drat *you*!"

If the foiled villain was looking for *curses!* he found a pretty good one in *drat*. Or at least he found a curse that hides a considerably harsher invective.

Drat sounds like the more modern exclamation, *rats!* (the plaintive expletive used by Charlie Brown of *Peanuts* fame), and its use is the same—to curse gently. But Charlie Brown, you're-a-good-man and all that, would never consciously curse either person or thing with "God rot it" or "God rot you."

Drat was formed from *'od rot*, the *'od* being *God*, and the *rot* transforming to *rat*, as was common in such word formation. This is similar to *God* being changed and disguised euphemistically in *egad*. In *egad* we find another softened exclamation: "a God!" or "by God!"

We have created myriad ways of disguising our breaking of the seventh commandment, "Thou shalt not take the name of the LORD thy God in vain," with *gosh* and *darn* and *goldarn* and *jeez* and *jeepers* and *criminy* and *Jiminy Cricket!* And with, of course, the more archaic exclamations of *drat!* and *egad!* Similar archaisms are *gadzooks!* and *zounds!* All those sound to today's ears like they should be displayed in cartoonish dialogue bubbles, but they represent softening of what in those days was some pretty severe cursing. *Gadzooks* is an alteration of "God's hooks," and *zounds* (once pronounced *zoonds*) is a shortening of "God's wounds" (the two oaths possibly references to Christ on the cross).

Gads, by the way, is short for "God save me." And if you're in a different mood, *Blimey!* (contracted from "God blind me").

Somewhat on the other side of the coin, what the dickens does "What the dickens?" mean?

What the deuce does "What the deuce?" mean?

Oh, what the hell, they mean ... well, they kinda mean "What the hell." Not the place, specifically, but the guy who runs it.

Both are euphemisms for *devil*.

fey

We are all, in a sense, fey. Not whimsical, otherworldly sort of fey, though some of us are that.

The "fated to die" sort of fey.

And I say "in a sense" in that *fey* in its original meaning (usage of which survives in Scotland) was "fated to die *soon*." May none of us be fey in that sense. Fates will bring us to the end, of course—may that end be a long way off.

The sense of whimsy or otherworldliness came about perhaps because some of those about to die exhibited abnormal behavior—superstition held that this was because the patient was possessed by unconventional forces, giving them powers of clairvoyance.

(The word *fey* in its current sense is often associated with fairylike qualities, though *fay* in relation to fairies is a quite distinct word. *Fey* is from an Old English word meaning "fated to die," while *fay* and *fairy* come to us through Old French from, ultimately, Latin *fatum*—ironically, "fate.")

Between whimsical now and in-throes-of-death then, *fey* also contained now-obsolete meanings of "portending death," "deadly," "cursed or unlucky," and "feeble or sick"—all seemingly associated with undesirable fates.

terrific

"Terrorists are terrific!"

I did not say this, and in fact that sentence is something that no one will ever say (not even as a slogan to recruit fanatics into murderous organizations). Yet it is true *in the original sense* of the now bizarrely redefined word *terrific*. Originally, something terrific frightened you. It caused terror. By the early 1800s the meaning had softened to communicate intensity, severity, or extremity, frightening or not. For example, a "terrific storm," meaning a large and powerful storm. By the early 1900s, *terrific* meant severely good. Same story for *awesome*, which went from "full of awe (reverence)" in the 1500s to "inspiring awe (fear or dread)" in the 1600s to "remarkable" in the 1960s to "Awesome, man!" in the 1980s. *Fearful* suffered such weakening, as well.

Terrible underwent similar softening (though *terrible* is a much older word, in use before 1400, while *terrific* was first recorded in 1667 in Milton). *Terrible* moved from "terrifying" (and "terrific") to "awful or bad" by the late 1500s.

Dreadful wandered down the same path from its Old English meaning of "filled with dread" by the early 1200s to "inspiring dread" a bit later to "awful or bad" by 1700. *Awful*—same thing. "Inspiring dread" and then "commanding respect" in Old English, to "majestic" by the mid-1600s to "egregious, bad" by the early 1800s. (And there are others—*horrible* is another good example.)

And the fact that powerful words can lose their meanings in this way is both terrible and terrible, dreadful and dreadful, awful and awful, horrible and horrible.

BaNe

Have you ever thought of someone—badgering boss, misbehaving teen, philandering lover—as "the bane of your existence"?

Better hope not.

Or you may not ever think that thought, or any other thought, again.

The original and now-obsolete meaning of *bane*, reaching back to Old English, was "killer or murderer," and later the killing itself.

The meaning broadened to anything that killed, including various poisons like ratsbane and wolfsbane, and then it became specific to poisons. By the late 1500s, the figurative meaning of "vexation, affliction, or anathema" had risen.

So in its original sense of the word, someone could be the bane of your existence only for a while, because you wouldn't be existing all that long.

spiLL

To hell with the clichés. Better start crying over spilled milk.

Mourn the spilling of milk. Sing dirges because of it. Weep openly.

To *spill* back in Old English was "to kill, slay, rob of life." (Stop me before I spill again!) And for several centuries of English it had associated meanings related to suicide, destruction, devastation, and spoilage.

By the early 1100s, to *spill* was "to ooze blood," a sense that led by the early 1300s to the meaning of *spill* as we know it.

Imagine, then, a cavalryman taking a spill from a horse … after either horse or rider had been spilled in battle.

SWELTER

It seems that the most common use of the verb *swelter* is in the nigh-unto-cliché phrase "sweltering heat." We don't seem to swelter much. We just suffer in the sweltering heat.

Such heat is, of course, quite miserable.

Not as miserable as it once was.

Swelter has echoes of *sweat* in it, and yes, we do sweat when we swelter.

Until we stop sweating. For instance, when we die.

To *swelt*, from way back in Old English, is "to die" (and later, "to kill"). By the 1300s, the word had softened to take on less deadly meanings of swooning or fainting. By the 1400s, the word was spelled *swelter* and had taken its present meanings of being afflicted by the heat: swooning or fainting or, yes, sweating.

Swelter has companions on its journey from fatal meanings to less intense meanings of suffering from circumstance or affliction. *Starve* followed that path. Like *swelt*, it originally meant "to die" or (later) "to kill." (It arose from an ancient Germanic root meaning "to be stiff.") As time went on, starving became associated with specific causes of death. By the 1600s, to *starve* could be "to die from or kill with hunger," or "to die from or kill with cold." The meanings related to cold themselves swelted and starved, leaving only the meanings related to hunger. *Starve*, like *swelt*, softened to take the meaning of being in a condition—lacking food—that will lead to death if not corrected.

RHYMES WITH "dead": CAUGHT READ-HANDED

WORDS OF CRIME AND PUNISHMENT

The words we discuss here will never caption a mug shot; nonetheless, they have criminal pasts. The forgotten crimes associated with them are years old—in some cases, hundreds of years old—yet in this chapter we diligently reopen the cases and ignore any etymological statutes of limitations.

Some of the crimes are current, though it's all in good fun—and fun, as you'll see, is one of those words playing a con game on us as we speak.

First, a note about the title of this chapter: "Rhymes With 'Dead': Caught Read-Handed." I confess that the reference to *dead* was to help readers (long E) to properly read (long E) past-tense *read* (short E).

But an even more appropriate justification of associating *dead* with *red-handed* becomes apparent in our first crime investigation (with punishment reserved for later).

Red-Handed

Caught red-handed? You're probably red-faced.

You're red-faced because you're embarrassed and blushing. The blood in your face is your own.

The blood on your hands is someone or something else's. Hands, after all, do not blush.

Being taken or caught "redhand" is a Scots legal term since the 1400s, and it's generally considered that the term comes from being caught with blood still on the hands. Suggestions have been made that this blood is from murder; others say poaching. Perhaps both. Blood is red no matter the type of animal that formerly contained it.

There is one speculation that the word may actually trace back to around 800 B.C., and an even more gruesome image, of guilt or innocence being tested by putting the accused's hand on a red-hot axhead.

fun

Cheating is fun. Swindling is fun. Deceiving is fun. Hoaxes are fun.

These are etymological and not moral declarations. A *fun* is, in the original meaning of the word, an instance of cheating, a swindle, a deception, a hoax.

The noun likely arose from the earlier verb meaning "to cheat or deceive" (by the late 1600s). This verb sense survives in the phrase "You're funning me." The noun sense survives in such phrases as "make fun of" or "poke fun at," basically connoting "make a fool of." Our modern usage of the noun *fun* as something that amuses, entertains, or delights began arising by the early 1700s (despite the fact that the renowned Dr. Samuel Johnson was not fond of it—he classified it as a "low cant word" in his 1755 *A Dictionary of the English Language*).

With this origin in mind, the "fun, fun, fun" in the Beach Boys song might be considered not the good times had driving that T-bird to the hamburger stand now, but the deceptive act of convincing the old man now that she's going to the library. The old man now was likely fond of his daughter (more so than Dr. Johnson was fond of the now-modern meaning of *fun*), as well the old man now should be in one sense of *fond*: Likely, the verb *fun* with the meaning of "to deceive" arose as an alternate pronunciation of the obsolete verb *fon*, "to be fool-ish" or "to make a fool of." If something fooled you, deceived you, you were *fonned*. And, therefore, if you are fond of something, you are, etymologically speaking, befooled by it. Once you're no longer fond of someone in that sense, it's time to take the T-bird away.

Hype

We continue to wallow in an age of hype. Ballyhoo about the latest blockbuster movie, the latest novel from a best-selling author, the latest music video from a controversial singer. Especially given the connection with vigorously promoting movies, one would expect that *hype* would be the result of some breathless headline writer for *Variety*, truncating the word *hyperbole* into the shorter and more-prone-to-screaming *hype*.

Hyperbole may indeed be a contributor, but another source is likely 1920s American slang.

As a slang word, *hype* in the 1920s had a couple of different meanings, likely from different formations. There's *hype* the short-change artist, a cheat who gives you change for a ten when you gave him a twenty. No one knows how that word came about (though one suggestion is a shortening of the prefix *hyper-*, meaning "over"—do they mean something like the nonexistent word *hypercharger*?). Anyway, by the 1940s, to *hype* was "to cheat," and a *hype* was "an instance of cheating, deception, or other such conning." By the 1960s, the word was being applied to various types of vigorous musical record promotions, involving everything from payola to high pressure to pure hustle. The meaning is softer now, suggesting lots of exclamation points! and kiddie-meal action figures and star face time on the talk shows than true trickery.

The other *hype*, the one of *known* origin, was *perhaps* related. In the 1920s, a *hype* could also be a drug addict or an injection of drugs—or (and this is obviously the source of the word) the hypodermic needle that addicts use to inject. If you were on a drug high, you were *hyped up*. Excited. Maybe manic. Yearning to see blockbuster novels, read best-selling books, watch racy music videos. Of course, I'm kidding about the direct drugs-to-movies connection, but you can see how the slang word may have in some way contributed to shades of today's drumming-up-excitement meaning of the word. This is pure speculation, but perhaps the con artist hypes were drug addict hypes looking to pay for their habit (though such habits are usually not chump-change affairs).

(Neither word is likely related to *hyper*—"in a state of excitement or agitation." This is likely a truncation of *hyperactive*.)

patter

To *patter* in the early 1400s was originally "to breeze through a prayer quickly," especially the paternoster, or the Lord's Prayer (or perhaps I should say that the original meaning was "tobreezethroughaprayer-quickly"). Shortly thereafter, the verb also took the meaning of "prattle, babble, ramble on," and other meanings that I could patter through.

By the mid-1700s, the verb had been stolen and retooled as a noun. Well, not *stolen* exactly, but there were thieves involved, and we'll return to that factoid in a moment. The noun meaning of chatter and babble and prattling and rambling didn't arrive until around the mid-1800s. Backing up, it had taken the meaning of facile talk—as in the patter of a salesperson or a carny pitchman—by the late 1700s.

Patter as a noun arose as slang, to denote the jargon and slang used in criminal cant. Be assured that those folks used patter, but the fast one they were pulling was unlikely a quick repetition of the paternoster.

jack-in-the-box

The following story is real. The names have not been changed to protect the innocent.

Well, the story of the word is real, though the little tale I'm about to weave is fictional.

Imagine a Christmas morning. A youngster scrambles out of bed, heads for the tree and, yes, Santa has been there. The child opens the first present and finds … an empty box.

The parents of the child are appalled and shocked. They'd bought their young'n a jack-in-the-box, but it's gone. Who could have taken it?

Well, jack-in-the-box did it himself, of course.

The first jack-in-the-box was not a toy at all, but instead, a con man or—as Robert Nares describes in his 1905 *A Glossary of Words, Phrases, Names, and Allusions*—someone who "deceived tradesmen by substituting empty boxes for others full of money." That meaning was in use by the mid-1500s. By the early 1700s the word described a type of toy, the one that our woeful youngster did not get on Christmas morning because of the jack-in-the-box shenanigans of jack-in-the-box, names not changed to protect the innocent.

rookie

When I studied theatre in a previous century, I heard the tale of veterans (sophomores! wow!) who would play a trick on beginning students in the stagecraft and lighting classes. The translucent colored sheets placed on stage lamps to project different colors on scenes are called *gels*. The vets would hand a few gels to the beginner and ask him to wash these sheets. And better hurry—the director has demanded that they be in place for the rehearsal that starts in twenty minutes! Now, gels are so named because they were at that time made of gelatin. And gelatin dissolves in water—the colored gels dissolved in the hands of the panicked rookie.

The word *rookie* is likely a corruption of the word *recruit*, but it's very likely that it has some source in the slang word (in use by the late 1500s) for a con man or a cheat: *rook*. The rookie may very well have been the victim of the rook. That's an extension of a general term of disparagement of a person (by the early 1500s), which was in itself a figurative comparison to the disagreeable bird, the rook.

eLope

Imagine this scenario (women, please role-play with me here for a moment):

You're a family man, a husband, a father. One morning, you wake up to find that the young lady in your household has eloped. How romantic.

Don't try to tell your wife about it, though. She already knows. She is the one who ran away with her lover.

The original meaning of *elope* was legal (or, more pertinent to this discussion, illegal): to *elope* was to abandon one's husband for a lover. The more romantic notion of stealing away to get married (perhaps an independent borrowing from Dutch) came about in the 1800s. So men, if you marry anyone born *after* the 1700s, you have a greater chance of avoiding an elopement in your household.

pLagiarism

What writers don't regard their words as their children—precious, irreplaceable? And *plagiarism* is the kidnapping of their children. And I don't mean the words. I mean the little tykes, flesh-and-blood sons and daughters.

The root of *plagiarism* goes back to Latin *plagiarus*, the kidnapping of children and others to be sold into slavery. The word had added the figurative sense of literary theft by the early years A.D.; the poet Martial used it as such. (*Plagiarus* rose from *plagium*, the capture of game, which is perhaps also unfortunately applicable. Many of the authors who regard their words as their children should take a harder look—they'd see that their words are actually gamey beasts.) *Plagiarus* came to English in the early 1600s as *plagiary*, "one who plagiarizes," with both literal kidnapping and figurative wordnapping meanings. Tack on an English *-ism*, and you have *plagiarism*.

And you can mark my words. Then steal them. The beasts!

ORðeaL

No one wants to suffer through an ordeal. The taxing experiences we call ordeals try your patience, your durability, your ability to cope.

They once tried, in a legal sense, your criminal guilt or innocence.

And guilty or innocent, you would literally suffer through a literal ordeal.

If your wounds didn't fester after carrying a red-hot bar nine paces, you were innocent. Lucky you.

If you could retrieve a stone immersed in boiling water and didn't develop blisters, you were innocent. Lucky you.

If you managed to walk an obstacle course of nine red-hot plowshares without incurring injury, you were innocent. And, small detail: You had to do it blindfolded.

If you didn't drown after being thrown into a pool of water with a millstone tied around your neck, you were innocent.

These and other variations of ordeal (as in the phrase "trial by ordeal") lasted until the 1200s and were based on a concept called *judicia Dei*. If God protected you, allowing you to survive or remain scathed only to a certain degree, God was issuing His judgment of innocence. The weakened and nonlegal sense of *ordeal* had arrived by the mid-1600s.

Makes your daily ordeals a little less trying, doesn't it?

guy

Guys' night out. Get together with the guys. Be a nice guy. Let's go blow up the king. Guys' night out!

The Gunpowder Plot of 1605 was a foiled attempt, by a group of Roman Catholics, on the life of Protestant English King James I. The aforementioned gunpowder was to be employed to blow up the Houses of Parliament. Two and a half tons of gunpowder, it is said, were secreted into a chamber beneath the House of Lords. Authorities were alerted to the plot; they searched the chamber and captured the conspirator who was to have set off the gunpowder: Guy Fawkes. His compatriots were elsewhere in England, awaiting word of the assassination so they could take the next steps in their plan to bring a monarch more tolerant of Roman Catholics to power.

The assassination was to have taken place on November 5; today, throughout the old English Empire, people build bonfires and set off fireworks in celebration of the plot's failure (see also BONFIRE). Effigies of Guy Fawkes are dragged through the streets and thrown onto bonfires, as they have been for about two hundred years (for the two hundred years of the celebration before, the effigy was one of the Pope). The effigies are called *guys*. By the mid-1830s in England, *guy* was used pejoratively, referring to rough-dressed or otherwise grotesque men. By the late 1840s, *guy* had been taken up by us Yankees as a general term for a man, a fellow (and used to refer to women, as well, by 1940).

Now, if you want to really cringe about being one of the guys, or at least being Guido "Guy" Fawkes, look up the series of steps taken in the punishment Fawkes and his fellow conspirators were subjected to. The two elements of the descriptive phrase "drawn and quartered" refer to only two parts of the punishment. Not for the squeamish, and not for these pages. Fawkes could have only prayed for serving the punishment in effigy instead of in person. And believe me, his fellow conspirators did not enjoy being "one of the guys."

"you're so pretty," and other obnoxious insults

words of hidden deprecation, derogation, and degradation

Has someone called you nice? Shrewd and meticulous in your dealings? Prestigious?

Call the lawyer. That someone is insulting you—or at least the you that may have lived in previous lives.

All those thoughts are pretty complimentary, right? Wrong.

Which is why we begin our examination of the unwitting insult with:

pretty

Think you're pretty clever?

Think I'm being redundant in the sentence above? I am indeed being etymologically redundant by using the phrase "pretty clever." (And you're indeed pretty clever by spotting it.)

Pretty originally meant "artful, crafty, or cunning" in Old English, a meaning that is now obsolete. The word was not a compliment, having derived from a word that meant "wile or trick." Around 1400, *pretty* came to take such complimentary meanings as "admirable, fine, acceptable, honorable." And when it was applied in this sense to people, it was applied to males. The more female-specific sense of "fair, attractive" followed shortly behind, as did the more general sense, as in "a pretty sunset." The true adverbial use—meaning "rather"—was in place by the mid-1500s.

There is something of an insult in the modern sense of *pretty* in that it falls short of a full compliment. The person or sunset or whatever is not beautiful; it is almost that. This is the kind of partially hearted compliment that characterizes *ovation*.

So beware the pretty one; that person may be seeking to con you.

Nice

A word of warning: If you see or hear something too frequently, it begins to seem not familiar but alien, odd. So it will be with the word noted in the heading above.

Let's begin by looking at a few examples of using the flexible, complimentary, modern meanings of the word *nice*:

She's nice. She makes cookies.

That's a nice restaurant. Patrons must dress up to go there.

Nice job! Adroitly accomplished, with panache.

And you are nice. You put up with all these variations of the present use of the word *nice*.

But let's revisit this word in the context of its origins and its changes in meaning over the years.

You are nice. You're ignorant of the original meaning of nice. The source of English *nice* was an Old French word meaning "ignorant." Well, *ignorant* is too harsh a word. After all, the origin of *nice* is itself nice (as in, not obvious).

Let's look at our other examples with similar historical synonymy:

She's nice. She's screwing the neighbors. (Apparently luring them into her boudoir with those home-made cookies.) *Nice* in its earliest English meaning was "wanton."

She's nice. She refuses to go to any restaurant except the finest ones. And she won't go unless she can dress nicely. She's being persnickety about her restaurant choice, and when she does go, she wants to dress a bit garishly.

You're nice if you take her to that fine restaurant. She's going to order the most expensive dishes. *Nice*: stupid, foolish. And if she eats all she orders, she may not be nice anymore. *Nice*: "slender." But if you don't take her, she will be nice when considering your commitment to her. *Nice*: "doubtful, critical."

I know that you want me to go on and on with such examples but I, too, am nice. Not *nice:* agreeable, but *nice:* unwilling.

After all, as the saying doesn't go, "nice word, if you can get it."

SHREWD

Let's assume you're a shrewd judge of character and of the world in general. You're astute, sagacious, savvy, and perceptive.

You can immediately identify good qualities in a person or a situation. And you can as easily spot the bad: malicious, wicked, evil, harmful, irksome, vile, hurtful, adverse, dangerous, ill-tempered, unfavorable, ominous, harsh, in disorder, ugly, severe, shrewish, abusive, depraved, unsatisfactory, ugly, mean-tempered, scolding, naughty.

If you see these qualities in the persons or situations or things you are evaluating (and of course, if you are correct), you are shrewd. So are they.

Shrewd has over the years meant all those things, variously applied to people and animals and children and things. Only by the 1500s did positive senses of the word begin to arise, and now we are left only with the positive.

But I'll bet you can never again look at *shrewd* without seeing *shrewish* or, for that matter, the animal the *shrew*, very likely the source of the word, transferred to denote a mean man, from which the adjective developed.

BLUNt

An ironic synonymic phrase for *blunt* is "to the point."

So let's be pointedly blunt: Originally (twelfth century, or thereabouts), a blunt person was stupid. A dullard. Unable to perceive; unable to think. A quick and not necessarily etymologically precise series of connections: Dull person became figuratively dull object, like a blunt instrument. Using a blunt instrument is indelicate. A blunt person, who can be very sharp indeed in both perception and ability to think, is indelicate.

Straight to the point: Calling a person blunt is etymologically calling her stupid.

fastidious

If you're fastidious (in the modern meaning in use since the early 1600s), you're exacting, persnickety, quick to disgust, attentive to details. But not attentive enough. One detail you may have missed is the one that should disgust you: Around the mid-1400s, *fastidious* meant "haughty, disdainful." It comes from Latin *fastidiosus* ("disdainful, exacting"), which in turn comes from *fastidium* ("loathing"). *Fear and Fastidium in Las Vegas.*

By the early 1500s, if you were fastidious, you could be disgusted. You could also be disgusting, the source of disgust. (Though these meanings are now obsolete, I submit that if you're *too* fastidious, you're in danger of being disgusting, even today.)

meticulous

When this book is typeset, I will proofread it meticulously, fearing that I will find errors.

In the original sense of *meticulous*, I could very well be reading it nonchalantly, skimming here and letting my mind wander there, but still be meticulous, still fearful.

Fearful and timid and laden with dread were the first meticulous people. If one is fearful, one might be more apt to pay attention to details. If one is neurotic, like I am, he can sometimes be so fearful that he pays far too much attention to details, and by the early 1800s, that was also a meaning of *meticulous*. The modern, positive sense of being careful to good end arose later.

So, if you know someone who's meticulous, don't make any sudden movements.

deft

Deft has fairly meek and gentle origins, but we'll apply some guilt by association to it. One person being daft doesn't mean that person's sibling is daft too, despite common parentage.

That said, *daft* has meek and gentle origins, as well.

Deft and *daft* ultimately are the same word—*deft* is a form of *daft*, both meaning, yes, "meek and gentle." But the two words, both from before the 1200s, parted ways very early on: *deft* by the 1400s taking on its present meaning (and deftly so) and *daft*, quite undeftly and quite daftly, wandering from meanings of "silly" to "stupid" to (by the 1500s) "daffy."

And peek a bit more closely at brother *deft*, and you find a skeleton in that familial closet. *Deft* for a brief time around the 1400s was used to mean "stupid."

giddy

If you're really jovial, you might become giddy. And who knows, Roman god Jove himself might be what caused it.

These days, *giddy* means "figuratively drunk with exhilaration or elation," a sense that had arisen by the mid-1500s. Moving back through time, the word also meant "causing dizziness," as would something swirling about, and "vertiginous"—meanings arising in the 1500s. But the original meaning of *giddy* in Old English was something a bit more intense than just loopy with excitement. It meant "insane" or just plain "stupid." The word likely implied possession by a god (and is likely related to an Old Teutonic word, *gudo*, meaning "god").

If you're giddy about something, you're affected by *enthusiasm*—once again, possession by a god.

BRaVeRY

You have to compliment the word *bravery* for its bravado. *Bravery* makes a fine show of its respectable qualities, its courageous meaning, its admirable image. But that fine show of bravado may just be hiding some doubt. That fine show may be covering something up. It may be false.

And indeed it is.

Bravado is "boasted, ostentatious courage, perhaps false."

Bravery is "boasted, ostentatious courage, perhaps false," as well.

Bravery (brought over probably from French by the mid-1500s) originally meant what *bravado* means to us today: a bragging show of courage, bluster. The word was quickly used in its positive, respectable, and admirable sense by the late 1500s.

By the way, the ultimate origin of *brave* as an adjective is not certain. Given some of the speculations, we can understand the bravado of the word *bravery*; it knew well its hidden past (even though we don't). The word was borrowed from French, which brought it in from Italian, but at that point the suggested sources begin varying. Suffice it to say that the now-respectable word *brave* may have come from roots with less respectable meanings, including "wild" or "villainous" or "barbarian."

friend

"Gonna be home late tonight, honey. Having drinks with a friend."

Uh-oh. Call the divorce lawyer.

The word *friend* has held various meanings of convivial companion or ally from its very beginning, but for a time, *friend* meant "lover."

If your significant other and the "friend" are genial, go ahead with the appointment with the divorce lawyer once you've called. *Genial* is an adaptation of Latin *genialis*, which comes from *genius*, which is ultimately from a Latin root form of *gignere*, meaning "to beget." In fact, *genial*, when it came into English by the mid-1500s, meant "related to marriage, nuptial" or "related to generation and growth" (the modern meaning arose by the mid-1700s).

So if you get that "having genial drinks with a friend" call, the heck with the lawyer. There's going to be etymological begetting and marriage going on. You might instead respond by employing a friend in a nineteenth-century meaning: "a duelist's second."

NOSY

Nosy people figuratively stick their noses into places they don't belong, such as in other people's business. If the nosy people meddle during such intrusions, they are also considered busybodies. And it is one part of the physical body that, in the original meaning of *nosy*, is being busy.

That part will surprise you.

Well, no it won't. That part is, of course, the nose. Calling someone nosy was once an insult of a physical and not a behavioral characteristic. A nosy person had a big schnozz. Cyrano de Bergerac was a nosy person even though he minded his own business (well, his and Christian's and Roxanne's). This use, though not common, predated our slang use of *nosy* by about three hundred years and is first recorded in the early 1600s. More commonly, since the 1700s, *nosy* was a nickname for a schnozz-enhanced person.

So if you call someone nosy, beware when that person turns to face you. You might just get knocked flat with that beak.

paNts

Growing old should not scare the pants off you. It should scare the pants onto you.

If you wear pants, you are sporting a garment that has its origins in buffoonery and farce, and that specifically makes stereotyped skinny old people look more ridiculous.

The word traces back to commedia dell' arte, an old Italian theatre form (beginning in the 1500s) combining improvisation and standard bits actors could weave in at appropriate moments. One of the stock characters in this theatre form was Pantalone, a mean, miserly merchant and a bit of a dirty old man. He was frequently portrayed stooped over from age.

The Pantalone character wore tight-fitting trousers or leggings. Trousers like those worn by Pantalone were called *pantaloons* in the 1600s, and by the 1700s the word was applied to trousers (as opposed to knee breeches) in general. By the mid-1830s, the word had been shortened to *pants* (unrelated to the pants Pantalone did when leering at the female characters). So wear your pants knowing that they have their origins in making light of old folk (in fact, by the 1600s the word *pantaloon* meant "old codger"). And men, keep your pants on lest you be accused of being a dirty old man like the commedia dell' arte dirty old man. (Particularly good advice for the Brits, where pants are underwear.)

senate

Given the lineage of the word *pants* (see above), I suggest that the appropriate dress code in the U.S. Senate—or in any Senate, for that matter—would indeed be pants. (And maybe shoes and shirts and that other stuff, too.)

Pants ultimately derives from a parody of old men, while *senate* has a more direct lineage from "old men." The word *senate* comes to us through French from Latin *senatus*, "council of old men." Yes, the word is male-specific to rile both the feminists and the advocates of seniors. Particularly that last group, as the root of senate (*sen-*) also gave us *senior* and *senile*.

Now, if we could only talk the old men in the Senate into keeping their pants on.

teen

Anyone who has raised teens understands that stage where your children want to have nothing to do with you. They might even go as far as to deny their parentage.

That gives us absolutely no connection to the word *teen* itself. *Teen*, short for *teenager*, would itself deny its parentage to the obsolete word *teen*, meaning "mischief, affliction, annoyance, anger, and vexation, or the source of annoyance, trouble, or vexation."

In this case, denial of parentage is entirely accurate. The obsolete *teen*, from an Old English word meaning "injury," has absolutely nothing to do with the modern *teen*, ultimately from the suffix *-teen*, used to denote the addition of ten. So its inclusion in a list of hidden word origins is cheating, I readily admit, but for all you moms and dads out there, the connection to "source of vexation" seems so accurate, doesn't it?

coax

To seduce someone is to coax them. Perhaps in more ways than one.

Various meanings of *coax* have been around since the late 1500s, but the original sense seems to be "deceive, make a fool of." Specifically, to coax is "to make a cokes" of someone—a *cokes* being a fool. (*Cokes* may be an insult to Cockneys, by the way.)

Now, there are some seducers who are indeed coaxers in this sense. A good pickup line, a few stretches of the truth (vocational, marital, and physical), and the seducer has indeed coaxed.

Another meaning of *coax*, obsolete as well, is "to caress or fondle." Certainly a good bit of that sort of coaxing in a successful seduction.

These senses have died out, leaving the modern sense of the word, the sense most applicable to a lot of clumsy seducers—persuasion by wheedling, flattery, pleading, and persistence.

CONCiERGE

In the American hotel industry, the concierge is the person who assists guests with travel arrangements, transportation, reservations, and the like. The concierge is something of a gatekeeper at the hotel, and in fact the word has origins in keeping an eye on the front door.

Concierges are generally helpful and eager to assist. Don't treat them like slaves, though.

Even though, etymologically, that's probably what they are. The probable ultimate source of *concierge* is Latin *conservus*—"fellow slave."

Conservus is not a pun on "come serve us," but the wordplay is irresistible. Concierge! Come serve us!

ethnic

Calling someone a dummy insults more than one person; there's the direct target of the insult as well as the secondary target—the source of the phrase, based on the stereotyped and incorrect assumption that someone who is dumb (who can't speak) is stupid.

Some double insults are obvious. *Gyp* (meaning "to swindle") is an example of a well-hidden insult based somewhat on ethnicity: *gyp* is a shortening of *gypsy*, which is itself an alteration of *Egyptian*.

An even more-hidden example of the ethnic insult is *ethnic* itself. The word as an adjective, in use by the late 1400s (the noun was in use by the late 1300s), meant "not Judeo-Christian." In other words, using the word *ethnic*, you're etymologically insulting people of other religious backgrounds in the context that they are pagans or heathens.

Our current meaning of *ethnic*—a people or nation or otherwise distinguishable group within a larger group—comes from the twentieth century.

Husky

A husky is a dog, right?

Well, a husky dog is a dog. A *husky* is an Inuit—an Eskimo. Or at least that's what the word *husky* meant in its original use. *Husky* was a corrupted pronunciation of *Eskimo*. A husky dog, then, was a dog used by the huskies, and the shortened phrase has come to mean the dog itself. (As a side note, *husky* meaning "big, sturdy" is unrelated—it refers to having a constitution as strong as that of a corn husk. *Husky* applied to the voice, meaning "dry, raspy," is of the same agrarian origin—the voice is as dry as corn husks. Not in themselves insults, but such origins do call to mind images of scarecrows.)

Pidgin

Let's get down to business: There's a temptation to make fun of people who stumble through a second language. They get the accented syllables wrong, they garble the grammar, they sprinkle in words from their language or other languages, they struggle to find the word or group of words that might communicate their thoughts, they mangle pronunciations. So, to communicate without a fully mastered common language—as the nineteenth-century Chinese and British traders had to do—a simplified version of a language is created. This version of the language is called a *pidgin* or *pigeon.*

Now, the compassionate readers of this book, I know, would not even think about making fun of someone who uses a pidgin in attempts to communicate—except when you use the word *pidgin*, you've unknowingly engaged in something of a mockery.

Specifically, *pidgin* was used by the mid-1800s to describe the English spoken by the Chinese in the business of trading. By the late 1800s, the word had extended to cover any simplified language spoken to communicate with another who doesn't share a first language—that is, a lingua franca.

But the insult to the Chinese is not simply that the word was applied to them specifically. There is another insult. *Pidgin* was the English-speakers' "translation" of the way the Chinese pronounced the word *business.*

puckish

Puckish describes those with a mischievous, impish, almost charmingly playful quality. It's a cute word, and we've been using it since the late 1800s.

The original puck wasn't so cute.

In Old English, *puca* was a demon. In Middle English the *pouke* was the Devil himself, and a puck could be an evil person.

prestige

People with prestige have a bit of magic about them. Status, track record, respect, honor, an important job. And such people would be shocked to know that all that prestige is a facade, an illusion, a deceit. In the original sense of the word, anyway. And whatever title they hold, whatever role, whatever calling, they will never have as much prestige as the lowly magician.

Prestiges in the 1600s were tricks, illusions, particularly those of jugglers and conjurers. You can see the word *prestige* in a word for the magician's art—*prestidigitation*. These words have mutual origins through French from Latin, ultimately from a phrase meaning "blindfold the eyes."

By the early 1800s, *prestige* had taken on senses of "glorious image or reputation" (to the point of being blinding) and further softened in the 1900s to today's meaning of "respected status, reputation, esteem."

Didn't see all that trickery when looking at *prestige*? Not surprising: The word *prestige* has performed a prestige.

mascot

You're likely familiar with your favorite teams' mascots. Some examples:

- for the Wisconsin Badgers, Bucky the French Witch

- for the Cleveland Indians, Chief Wahoo the French Witch

- for the Orlando Magic, Stuff the Magic French Witch

The word *mascot* comes from French *mascotte*, "sorcerer's amulet or charm." The word took international life because of a nineteenth-century French comic operetta, *La Mascotte*, about Bettina, a woman who brings luck to a poor farmer—as long as she remains a virgin. *La Mascotte* premiered in Paris in 1880 and was so popular it crossed the English Channel to

London in 1881, and the Atlantic to Boston in 1882. Soon, *mascotte* (eventually taking the modern spelling) came into English meaning any kind of good-luck charm—people, animals, things, and eventually people dressed in fuzzy team character garb.

The French *mascotte* traces back to *masco*, or "witch" in Occitan (a language of Southern France)—in the case of the operetta that popularized the term, a good witch, but a witch nonetheless.

Team owners who are aware of the history of *mascot* and the operetta that helped popularize it would be wise to require the individuals dressed in those fuzzy mascot costumes to be virgins.

mask

Mascots (see above) sometimes wear masks—and there is likely an etymological connection between the two. The source of Occitan *masco*, "witch," may very well trace back to Medieval Latin *masca*, "mask, witch, specter, or nightmare." In turn, *masca* may have come from Arabic *maskhara*, "clown, laughingstock, buffoon." *Mask* may trace directly from *masca*, or from Italian *maschera*.

Wearing too much mascara can make one appear as if wearing a mask, or make one look like a buffoon, and mascara indeed was borrowed from Italian *maschera* or Spanish *mascara*, both meaning "mask." *Mascara* may ultimately trace back to the Arabic word for "clown or buffoon," as well.

pupiL

Students are likely more comfortable with their situations than pupils learning the same things.

Though *pupil* and *student* are considered synonyms today, the words have etymological differences, one minor but significant, the other, huge. The minor one first: Students study—that's obvious from the similarity of the words—and they have studied since the beginning of the word (by the late 1300s). Contextually, students are also taught. Pupils are taught, and contextually they also study. The difference here lies first in that the word *student* implies self-motivation, while *pupil* connotes tutelage (and there's certainly nothing wrong with that). By the mid-1500s, *pupil* meant one who is under the instruction of another, in the educational care of another.

But that meaning is an evolution of the original meaning of *pupil*, in use by the late 1300s. And herein lies the huge difference: A pupil was someone in a different situation, under a different sort of care.

A pupil was an orphan and a minor, and therefore a ward under the care of someone else.

So a student is more comfortable with her situation because she most likely still has parents.

spell—s-p-e-L-L, spell

Good students, even good pupils, are likely good spellers.

And if they're really good students or pupils, they will know that in the original sense of the verb *spell*, the phrase "good speller" is at best ironic and at most oxymoronic.

Originally, the verb *spell*, in use by the 1200s, meant "to read laboriously, to move through text with effort and difficulty." How do you fight your way through words and text that aren't immediately clear to you? *L-e-t-t-e-r b-y l-e-t-t-e-r.* (For a time, the word was used to describe laborious composition of text, as well.)

Clarifying the precise form of a word letter by letter as a meaning of *spell* arose by the late 1500s.

So, in the original meaning of the word, a person might have been forced to be a good speller because he was a damn poor reader.

exhuming the body

not-so-private conversations about private parts, bodily fluids, and sex

The body is buried in the words that follow, and we set about a path of exhuming. Autopsies of now-dead meanings. In doing so, we find some pretty public discussions of private parts, not to mention the entire human body itself. Breasts and bottoms and other things, and even an internal organ or two. All in our everyday speech.

Our discussion begins by revealing the full body and why we may never again walk into a gymnasium without blushing.

gymNasium

Most of us have put in due time on gymnasium floors, cheerleading or playing basketball or making clumsy attempts to dance suavely at prom time. Would our mothers have allowed such things if they realized that the ultimate source of the word *gymnasium* was the Greek verb *gymnazein*, meaning "to exercise naked"? Certainly variations of that concept of exercising naked were on the mind of many of those suave-hopeful young boys promming it up on the gymnasium floor, though I daresay that the thoughts were hardly etymological, and these couples likely wouldn't have been at the prom in the first place if they had told their parents that they were off to the dance at "the naked exercise place."

In direct defiance of *gymnasium*'s etymology is the attire men now wear in gym class—jocks. They've been around for a while: The word *jock* arrived in the 1920s as a shortening of *jockstrap*, from the late 1800s. But even before there were the athletic supporters we now refer to as *jockstraps*, there were the jocks that the straps strapped in—*jock* is slang for "penis" or "genitals." So even when the Greeks were exercising naked, they were sporting jocks, each and every one.

And while we're on the subject of proms—and bodies ...

corsage

Prom time.

Compliment your friend's date on her beautiful corsage. Get slapped by the young lady if you're a man; get an odd look if you're a woman. Get punched by your friend (he's a mean cuss and doesn't treat men or women differently).

You have specifically complimented your friend's date on her beautiful "bouquet de corsage," the French phrase for the floral arrangement she wears on her bust, apparently shortened in the early 1900s by removing the word *bouquet,* which is the word sporting the core meaning. *Corsage* in the 1400s was stature and size of the body, kind of a physical complement to the word *carriage* in the bodily sense. By the 1500s, it came to mean the body itself, the torso (as opposed to the arms and legs), as well as the upper body—and the bust. By the 1800s, the word had wandered to the meaning of clothing for the corsage—*corsage* meant "bodice" (the French *corsage* shares a root with *corset*). And by the turn of the century, it was the bouquet worn on that bodice.

It probably never had the same effect of "Hey babe, nice rack!" but if you're complimenting a member of the opposite sex on his or her body (his or her corsage), you'd better watch your choice of flowery words. Or your fiery and jealous friend might help you find the original root for the word, the Latin *corpus*, from which we got *corpse*.

jock

In the entry for *gymnasium* (see above), I discussed jockstraps and the fact that we've mostly forgotten that these straps strap in *jocks*, eighteenth-century slang for genitals. I admit that in that discussion I was being a mite sexist. I didn't point out that the slang word originally referred to either female or male genitals.

There are, therefore, unknown etymological degrees of insult when referring to an athlete as a jock: (1) the common and prevalent meaning of being devoted completely to sports and oblivious to the rest of the world (okay, a nice way of saying "stupid"); (2) the largely forgotten meaning of being a male organ (okay, a nice way of saying "dickhead"), and at its lowest level; (3) the obsolete meaning of possibly being female genitals (and I'm not going to venture any un-nice meanings for that).

cul-de-sac

It takes guts to live in a cul-de-sac.

Blind guts to be exact. The caecum, for instance, which is the first part of the colon (your appendix, if you still have one, is attached to it). The caecum is a cul-de-sac (French for "bottom of the bag or sack"), or a blind gut, because there is only one opening to it. By the 1800s, the term came to be used for both figurative and literal dead ends, such as the street that ends in a circle. And speaking of ends, dead or otherwise, *cul* in French is said to be a bit ruder version of the euphemistic English use of *bottom*.

HUMOR

You are a humorous person. So's your mom. And your dad. Grandparents, too. All humorous. I know this for a fact.

How do I know? All people have humor.

Four humors, in fact.

All people, that is to say, have body fluids, which were called humors in Middle English. Black bile and yellow bile and phlegm and blood, all sloshing about and making you what you are.

At first, the humors were thought to control the body's health. Blood strengthens and colors the body. Phlegm moistens it. Choler (yellow bile) aids body heat and the senses. Melancholy (black bile) nourishes the bones and balances blood and choler. Belief in the humors' control of the body was extended by the late 1400s to belief in their controlling disposition, then by the early 1500s in their controlling mood. If your body had black bile in excess, you suffered melancholia. Heavy on the phlegm—phlegmatic, of course. A bit too much yellow bile, and you had a temper (and eventually, gall). Blood overbalance? You're sanguine. One of the moods supposedly caused by the balance of humors was one of fancy and whimsy (a use from the middle 1500s), and by the late 1600s, humor in the sense of something that causes laughter had arrived.

But tell someone today that your moods are dictated by phlegm and black and yellow bile, and they'll likely laugh at you. You're humorous, after all.

HECTIC

Is the feverish pace of today's hectic life wearing you down? Even so, you will likely prefer it to the hectic life of yesteryear—and the hectic death of those times, as well.

Hectic, in use by 1400, was a medical term describing the fever and other habitual symptoms of consumptive diseases, such as tuberculosis. It was first spelled *etic* or *etyk* after being adapted from Old French *etique*, but in the 1500s, the modern spelling arose by association with the source of *etique*—Latin *hecticus*.

Medical fever was transferred to figurative fever, first recorded in Rudyard Kipling's *Traffics and Discoveries* (1904). So, though we live in hectic times, we are more likely to survive them than were the sufferers of the original hectic symptoms.

Nostalgia

There is no nostalgia for the original meaning of *nostalgia*. No longing for nostalgic times, no fond memories of nostalgic people.

Because, you see, nostalgia was considered a medical condition. An affliction. A severe reaction to being in unfamiliar surroundings—homesickness in the literal sense. And indeed, when you break the word into its component parts, you find homesickness. The *-algia* comes to the word through the same medical construction as *neuralgia* (*-algia* indicating pain). And Greek *nostos* means "journey to or arrival at home." *Nostalgia* in this sense was in use in English by the mid-1700s, borrowed likely from a 1688 medical treatise by Swiss physician Johannes Hofer, *Dissertatio Medica de Nostalgia, oder Heimwehe* (*Medical Dissertation on Nostalgia, or Homesickness*). The treatise is written in Latin, though *Heimwehe* is German for "home-pain." Sea-farers and soldiers far from home suffered the disease, characterized by such symptoms as despondency, melancholia, palpitations, and emaciation. The word was shedding its medical sense in the 1800s (though the concept was still being discussed in medical journals in the 1860s, related to Civil War afflictions). By 1900, we were using the figurative sense of fond memories, or of longing or pining.

fascinate

If you were to—for whatever reason might impel you to be tossing insults about—call someone a witch, prepare to be fascinated by the response. Unless you can ward the witch off with your phallus.

By the late 1500s and until the mid-1600s, to *fascinate* was "to bewitch or charm with magical spell." It also held for a time the meaning of, loosely, "to hold fast with a look or an evil eye," usually applied to magical snakes. (Fans of Harry Potter and Dungeons & Dragons will recognize this power in the mythical basilisk.) The connotations of literal magic slipped away, so that by the mid-1600s you could be fascinated—robbed of resistance or chance to escape—figuratively by someone or something great and powerful. And about the same time, you could be fascinated in the modern sense—held intellectually fast by something interesting or in some other way exciting.

Fascinate ultimately arises from the Latin *fascinum*—"witchcraft or spell." One of the spells that the ancient Romans sought to cast was one to ward demons and ill spirits. They sought to accomplish this with a charm, a talisman, a symbol: a phallus. Apparently, the sexual symbolism thereof represented a counter-magic for the Romans. Writes Reay Tannahill in *Sex in History* of one example: "The Roman God Liber ... was generally represented by a phallic symbol, which stood not only for sex but conquest, defiance, and protection against the evil eye—a kind of magical, multipurpose obscene gesture." A later (and minor) Roman phallic god was named Fascinus.

shape

"The shape of things to come" is a cliché, it is a phrase forming the title of an H.G. Wells novel, and it is, unintentionally, a pretty ribald pun if you look back into Old English and apply some modern slang.

Shape has had many meanings over the centuries and in fact had many meanings in its very infancy. Round and triangular and cylindrical are all shapes (an Old English sense). You can be fit—in good shape (in use by the mid-1600s). Things can take form, take shape (also in use by the mid-1600s). And on and on and on.

But let's return to "round and triangular and cylindrical are all shapes"—and another unintentional pun, this time visual. Another meaning of shape in its Old English infancy was "sex organs." (A whole new perspective on the adjective *shapely*, is it not?)

Round and tri ... um ...

"The shape of thi ..." um ...

Time to move onto the next entry before we lose our PG rating.

VERGE

The word *verge* traces back to Latin *virga,* or "rod." By the late 1400s, after having been used to describe other things (about which, more in a moment), the word *verge* meant "a staff, rod, or scepter that symbolizes rank or office." The phrase "within the verge" by the early 1500s denoted the lands within the jurisdiction if the English Lord High Steward—that is, within the figurative sweep of the rod that symbolized the Lord High Steward's authority. By the 1600s, *verge* was used synonymously with *border*, since "within the verge" or "outside the verge" communicated the same thoughts as "within the border" or "outside the border."

Now, let's wander back to a brief but first-recorded use of the word *verge* sometime before 1400.

Verge meant "penis"—a different sense of the Latin word for "rod" (in some situations more so than others).

Verge also later meant a type of architectural column and a type of candle. Again, we see the relation to rod.

By the late 1700s, *verge* was borrowed from French to mean the sex organ of male mollusks and other invertebrates. I've never seen a male mollusk sex organ, so I'm unable to comment on the clarity of its relation to "rod."

Now, the original fourteenth-century meaning of *verge* as "penis" gives a whole new perspective on the concept of coitus interruptus, which—depending on how far along things are—would stop activities when someone was "on the verge"—he figuratively, she literally.

Though watch your meanings—sex with a mollusk is a bit kinky.

PENCIL

By the early 1900s, *pencil* was used as slang for "penis." This is notable because the ultimate source of the word *pencil* is … *penis*.

Penis is a Latin word meaning exactly what it says, but it also meant "tail" (and the anatomical meaning may have been a slang reference to the meaning of "tail"). A *peniculus* in Latin was a brush (a little tail) and a *penicillus* was a paint brush, and with spelling variations the word *pencil* came to English through French by the early 1300s. And in fact the earliest meaning of *pencil* was "a finely tapered paint brush." The modern usage rose in the 1500s.

So if you jot that down, maybe you'd better use a pen.

This next note, however, you could more safely jot in pencil. Another word that traces back to *penicillus* (which traces back to *peniculus* and ultimately *penis*) is the scientific name for a type of mold with brush-like asexual sporing structures: *Penicillium notatum*. This mold is, of course, the source of the antibiotic penicillin. Odd that penicillin is used to treat some "social diseases" like syphilis and gonorrhea, which are also associated with that oft-mentioned-above Latin root word.

Now, if you believe that all this has nothing to do with the source of the word *peninsula*, often shaped like ... well, you know ... you'd be absolutely right. The roots of *peninsula* mean "almost-island" and have nothing to do with brushes and tails and other things.

ORCHID

Flower arrangers don't know this, but the most appropriate way to display orchids may be to cover their roots in fig leaves, so you can't see them (not that you can see them anyway, at least while planted). With orchid roots thusly covered, the overly sensitive won't object to such a florally wanton display; they won't complain to the local keeper of decency laws, won't call the police, won't picket your home.

The way they might if you were displaying the statue of David and other other artwork depicting anatomically correct males.

How to stop the protests against Michelangelo's *David*? The discreet fig leaf.

The orchid is a plant in the family *Orchidaceae*. (It matters not to this discussion what family fig leaves are from.) *Orchidaceae* ultimately traces back through Latin to a Greek word literally meaning "testicle." Orchid roots—if you peek, you naughty botanist you—apparently impressed someone as resembling testicles.

The Greek origin made it even more literally to English, by the way. As in *orchidectomy*. I don't think I have to give the definition of that word—and I'll spare the male readers the involuntary flinching that would result were I to give it.

galoot

We'll cut this one short. No one is sure where the word *galoot*—a kind of likable oaf—comes from, but one theory is that it is derived (but not shortened, ironically) from Dutch *gelubt*. Eunuch.

(Theories that the word derived from a yelp of pain when trying to pronounce *orchidectomy* [see ORCHID] are unlikely, not to mention completely made up just for the purpose of this aside.)

avocado

Not as pretty as orchids, but much better in guacamole, is the avocado. Orchids are mentioned here because of the origin of the flower's name, which is similar to the origin of the word *avocado*.

The word is ultimately from the Aztecs, who named the fruit *ahuacatl*. As we've seen elsewhere, body poetry is at work. *Ahuacatl* is the Aztec word for "testicle."

The Spanish in turn named the fruit with their word for "lawyer." Not because they thought their lawyers had balls, but because to the Spanish, *ahuacatl* sounded like *avocado* (in modern Spanish, *abogado*), "advocate or lawyer."

And to keep the males flinching at the thought of mashed testicles, the word *guacamole* had almost identical parentage—*ahuacamolli*, a compound word meaning "avocado sauce," was heard as *guacamole*.

if we only knew
what is issuing
from our mouths

words of bodily function
and dysfunction

"Say that again, and I'll wash your mouth out
with soap!"

It's a parental cry of a time gone by. And it was
easily evoked by young'ns speaking words that
were clearly identified as disgusting or taboo. The
S-word, primarily, but also the A-word and the
A-hole-word and the P-word (well, a couple of
those) and the H-word and especially (oh, do I

even hint at the first letter?) the letter-that-comes-after-E-word.

In those gone-by times, parents would have extended the cries had they but known the origins of the words their children were using—and that they themselves, along with etymologically gutter-mouthed Grandma and Grandpa, were speaking so wantonly. *If we only knew what is issuing from our mouths*—when in fact these words should be issuing from other parts of our bodies. On the pages that follow, we'll take a look at seemingly innocent words related to bodily functions and other such blushables, including:

- a different P-word
- a different S-word
- a different A-word
- and—of course!—a different letter-that-comes-after-E-word or two

We start with the previously threatened different P-word.

poppycock

Most curse words have four letters, they say.

And, with notable exception, that is indeed true. Still, I respond, "Poppycock!"

Poppycock, you see, is one of those "dirty" words that have more than four letters. Instead of being a grandmotherly way to say "nonsense," it is ultimately a more gutter-minded way to say it. How so? As a caution against all you aspiring folk etymologists out there, the hidden offenders are not the syllable *cock*, and not the syllable *poppy* (yeah yeah, I'm sure we'll soon see some Internet post about how heroin poppies contributed to the etymology).

Pappekak is a direct import to English from a Dutch dialect, altered with a bit of American spelling. It means "soft dung." Therefore, *poppycock!* isn't any more polite than an exclamatory *horseshit!* (which, coincidentally, also does not have four letters).

Poppycock is first attested in 1865 and started out in the States. Location and timing allowed it to avoid a nonliteral bowdlerization (Bowdler didn't do it, but he would have) of several words that had the sensitive syllable *cock* in them. It's why we commonly call a male chicken a *rooster* instead of a *cock*, the metal silhouette of a cock sitting upon an arrow a *weathervane* instead of a *weathercock*, and that pile of dried grasses a *haystack* instead of a *haycock*. Other suggested victims include *abrecock* (now *apricot*, though the respelling is more likely by association with *abricot*, the French word for the fruit), *cockhorse* (now *rocking horse*), and the author of *Little Women*, Louisa May Alcox (technically Alcott, since her father as a youth changed the family name perhaps in this embarrassed fervor from Alcox). Hitchcocks the country over were blushing. (Words like *titbit,* changed to *tidbit,* exhibit similar squeamishness.)

mist

Years ago, a game called *Myst* ruled the computer gaming market, spawning four sequels and a spoof called *Pyst*.

The makers of *Pyst* were seeking parody, not accuracy, but managed to achieve both.

Mist in English has always meant just that. Water vapor. And many languages feature *mist* cognates or similar words meaning clouds. These words ultimately trace back to an Indo-European root, *meigh-*, meaning "to urinate."

Pissy weather, indeed.

fizzLe, part i

Listen carefully. Shh. Be very quiet, and perhaps you can hear the original meaning of *fizzle.*

Say the word aloud. *Fizzle.*

Now shh.

Fizzle perhaps ultimately results from the same word-creation mechanism as the word *shh*—mimicking sound in words. Technically, onomatopoeia.

Fizzle. Can't you hear now the quiet passing of gas, the breaking of wind without the noise of breaking? To *fizzle*, from Late Middle English to the 1700s, was "to fart discreetly." In the 1800s, *fizzling* was "making a hissing sound." It's unclear if the etymology is direct, as the hissing sound might be related to *fizz* more than the original *fizzle*. Still, *fizz* may itself be related to the original *fizzle*.

Now, don't tell anybody about such a disgusting potential origin of the word *fizzle*. Shh!

fizzLe, paRt ii

Something that fizzles peters out at the end. End indeed—considering our discussion in part one above. "Peter out" is a bit of mid-1800s American mining slang whose origin is officially unknown. Speculation about origin falls into two camps, one of which is the mining camp. The *peter* in "peter out" is saltpeter (with origins in Greek *petros*, "rock"). When that ore is fully mined, it has petered out. The other camp—yes, you guessed it considering the context of our discussions here—is that the peter is French *péter*, to break wind. French *péter* is related to the archaic explosive device, the *petard*. Now that's *not* passing gas quietly.

feisty

Feisty means "irascible, temperamental, quarrelsome" or—more and more these days—"plucky, spunky, and tenacious."

And if you call someone *feisty*, and that person knows the origins of the word, you'll likely find out just how feisty that person is.

Feisty has roots similar to *fizzle* and *fizz*, and they go way back to Old English. *Fisting* in Old English was breaking wind. *Fist* is an instance of breaking wind. (A variant of *fist* is *feist*.) For a time, *fisting* was used in phrases to describe contemptible mongrels: "fisting dog," "fisting cur," as examples. Literally, a stinking, farting dog.

The word *feist* and the descendents of the canine pejoratives survive in American dialect as *feist*—"mongrel" dog. And such mongrel dogs tend to be temperamental. Feisty.

So if you have any feisty friends, buy them some deodorant.

partridge

It may come as a surprise to you that the partridge, seen mostly as a denizen of the pear tree in the classic Christmas carol, actually does live in the wild, as well. When the partridge is flushed in the wild (and perhaps from pear trees, as well), its wings apparently make a whirring sound. (Having never flushed a partridge in person, I can't describe it precisely.) Some have likened the sound of partridge taking wing to something of a fizzling sound, the sound of passing gas. Thus its name, tracing back through Old French through Latin through Greek to Proto-Indo-European itself, where *perd-* was a word base for "to fart." That's quite a length for gas to pass through. The fact that the first syllable of *partridge* rhymes with a certain rude word is not a coincidence.

So, when flushed, the partridge sounds not like it's taking wing, but like it's breaking wind.

pumpernickel

Please pass the pumpernickel.

Such an innocent request, and when we dig into the origins of *pumpernickel*, perhaps such a coincidentally rude one.

A certain level of "passing" is already going on in *pumpernickel*. This *pumper* is from the German word for passing gas, breaking wind. Originally an insult (one suggested etymology has *Nickel* meaning "bumpkin"; and another has it arising from Nickel, or Nicholas, the name of a goblin; and the *Oxford English Dictionary* has *pumpernickel* imported whole and unsliced from German, where it meant "lout" or "stinker"). So a pumpernickel was a farting rube, perhaps literally and perhaps figuratively. The insult by the mid-1700s apparently was redirected at this coarse bread, perhaps because it makes rubes fart.

soLuBLe

One problem people have faced likely since there were people in the first place is constipation. Constipation is not a soluble condition.

Soluble today means "solvable," such as a soluble problem, or "dissolvable," such as a soluble chemical. *Soluble*, *solve*, *dissolve*, and related words like *solvent* rise from the Latin *solvere*, "to dissolve or loosen."

Now, back to our fascinating discussion of constipation. Oh, you can solve the problem of constipation (meaning that it's a soluble problem), and the solution often involves taking solutions that will …

um ... dissolve the source of the condition facing you (or, more technically, facing *away* from you), meaning, again, that it's a soluble problem—in both modern senses of the word.

But if we are to be medically (and etymologically) precise, constipation is not a soluble problem in that if you were soluble in the first place, you wouldn't have constipation. When borrowed from Old French, probably in Late Middle English, *soluble* was a medical term applied to bowels that were relaxed and free of constipation. Constipation couldn't be solved or dissolved if the bowels were soluble, because there was no constipation in the first place.

However you look at it, *soluble* was first applied to our everyday art of defecation and later was applied to other more conversationally acceptable topics.

Lax

Worried that we're going to continue examining the disgusting after our discussion of *soluble*?

Relax!

Of course we are.

And we're going to continue with a word closely related to *relax*: *lax*.

Both ultimately derive from the Latin *laxus*, "loose." The looseness described when English adapted *laxus* around 1400 was bowel looseness—lax bowels operated properly, thank you very much. No need for a laxative.

That's the word's application to bowels. Now, if a *person* were lax, his bowels were working overtime. A bad thing. That sense, luckily, is now obsolete.

Subsequent meanings of *lax* followed, of course: "not strict" by around the mid-1400s, "slack" by the mid-1600s.

Relax, by the way, came to English independently of *lax*, despite its common source. To *relax* in English has always meant variations of "to reduce tension, to loosen, to slacken." *Relax* was formed in Latin as *relaxare*, from which we adapted it, and *relaxare* was formed from *laxus*.

Relaxation also rose ultimately from that source, through Old French. This word also had bodily connotations, which you should keep in mind when you next go on vacation seeking relaxation. Says *The Barnhart Concise Dictionary of Etymology*: "**relaxation** n. 1392 *relaxacioun* a rupture of some bodily part."

squirt

Once you discover the original meaning of *squirt*, you'll have second thoughts about squirting a little ketchup on your burger or a little mustard on your bratwurst. You'll probably also hesitate to call that cute kid next door "a little squirt," though that bit of slang probably already has a good amount of dust on it.

Squirt in its initial sense in the 1400s meant "diarrhea," a meaning that hangs around in the phrase "the squirts." To *squirt* was to let loose diarrhea, though early on it also had its present meaning, the one more compatible with thoughts of condiments.

fanny

It is perhaps one of the top ten classic quotes about language, and bears repeating: "England and America are two countries divided by a common language." Shaw, of course. And Oscar Wilde: "We have really everything in common with America nowadays except, of course, language."

The division can be worsened with inappropriate use of words with different meanings on each side of the pond. We're not talking about *elevator/lift* or *car hood/bonnet* or *truck/lorry* or *cotton candy/candy floss* or *bathroom/loo*.

Though we might pause on that last one and engage in a bit of bathroom discussion. Loo discussion for the Brits.

Anyway …

In the States, a bum is a lout or a hobo. In Britain, it's a backside, an arse. Not an ass. In Britain, an ass is a donkey (as in the literal jackass). In the States, an ass is a jerk (from the donkey sense) as it is in Merry Olde, or—as it usually *isn't* in Merry Olde—a backside. Not an arse. Ironically, Americans "soften" the word *ass* (with either derivation) by using *arse* as a euphemism (in our minds, this is the same as softening the word *goddamn* by saying *goldarn*) or as kind of a mock archaism (like when we revive *drat* for dramatic effect). The Brits would see the reversion of *ass* back to *arse* as intensifying the word. *Arse* has been the crude term for centuries, and by the mid-1800s the upstart spelling of *ass* came into use, causing confusion between the ass's arse and the ass's ass.

In the States, a euphemism for *ass* (bottom) is *fanny*. In Britain, only women have fannies, and fanny is fairly crude. This has some dire implications for the American strapped-on tote bag, the fanny pack, and makes Little Annie Fanny, a recurring cartoon strip in *Playboy*, all the more suggestive.

A non-Brit might get confused about fannies, and become a bugger. Both sides of the pond use this word in soft terms, as in "Isn't he a cute little bugger?" but those eastward have a greater awareness that the word also means "sodomite."

In the States, *beaver* is a euphemism for what the Brits call a fanny. In Britain, to "beaver away" is to work diligently (be busy as a beaver). In working hard, the Brits will try to keep their pecker up—keep their resolution in mind, synonymous with "stiff upper lip." In the U.S., men will try to keep their pecker up (and stiff, too) in quite a different context.

In the States, if you're pissed, you're angry. In Britain, you're drunk. In either place, if you're one you could very likely be the other.

Chris Rae runs a Web site called The English-to-American Dictionary (http://english2american.com). He writes, "One of the most amusing e-mails I've had concerning this page was from an American who had arrived at her company's U.K. offices to be told that the person she was looking for was 'outside blowing a fag.'" In the U.K., smoking a cigarette. In the U.S. ... um, something different.

Of course, it's not like the Americans and the Britons don't speak with each other and are totally unaware of these differences. As Rae writes about the phrase "knocked up": "In U.K. English, knocking someone up involves banging on their door, generally to get them out of bed. In U.S. English, knocking someone up is getting someone pregnant. However, although most Brits will feign innocence, most of us do know the U.S. connotations of the phrase and it adds greatly to the enjoyment of using it." In the U.K., banging on the door. In the U.S., banging something else.

Rae also notes of "beaver away": "these days you'd have difficulty saying it without a chorus of sniggers from the peanut gallery, as we also all know the American definition. It's the sort of thing your grandmother might say at Christmas dinner that would make the younger generations choke on their soup."

By including the observation that a lot of times we really know what the other-siders mean, I don't mean to blow off the importance of knowing the differences in the dialects, especially because in the U.S., to blow something off is to ignore it. In the U.K., to blow off is to pass gas. (I wonder what the Brits, then, think of the phrase "to blow off steam." That's gotta hurt!)

mistLetoe

Mistletoe has nothing to do with missiles (nor with toes, for that matter), though the missile homonym has a certain ironic connection.

A Christmas tradition has lads and ladies smooching under the mistletoe, but they'd better not stand there for long, lest a bird crap on them.

Mistletoe is a compound word meaning "mistle-toe twig" (in that *mistle-* comes from *mistil*, which in itself means what *mistletoe* means to us today). *Mistil* arises from a Proto-Germanic root that Craig M. Carver (in *A History of English in Its Own Words*) notes leads to Gothic and Old High German words for dung; *The American Heritage Dictionary of the English Language* traces the word back to the Indo-European root *meigh-*, meaning "to urinate" (the source of MIST).

So, we have a word based on the bathroom habits of birds—because the plants tended to grow where there were a lot of droppings. This wasn't immediately connected with the fact that there might be seeds in those droppings, and mistletoe, it's said, was believed to spontaneously generate from the dung (the same way that flies generated spontaneously from garbage). This power to give life to plants made it a symbol of fertility, leading to its use in wedding ceremonies, where more than kissing was eventually involved.

Just watch out for those bird missiles.

(The toe part of *mistletoe* results from the sort of confusion that has led to many word constructions over the centuries. The word originally was *mistiltan*, *-tan* meaning "twig." But in Old English, the word was confused as being a plural, the way that *child* and *brother* are made plural in *children* and *brethren*. We have the same problem today with singular words that end in -*s*, such as the singular word *kudos*. *Tan* is the plural of *ta*, and *ta* means "toe." You say potata, I say potatoe—apropos of nothing but a bit of wordplay.)

addled

Does all this discussion of bathroom meanings of words leave you a bit addled?

It should. Here's why: You may have heard the insult "he has shit for brains." There's a quick way of expressing nearly the same thought, a way more common and more publicly voiced: "He's addled."

Addle as a noun has been with us since Old English. It means "stinking urine" or in some senses "liquid feces" or other disgusting liquids. Its use became limited to the phrase "addle egg," a rotten egg that won't hatch. The Greeks called this a "wind egg"—it had been fertilized by the wind. Wind egg, brought into Latin, is *ovum urinum*, a term corrupted in medieval Latin (illiteracy? carelessness? cleverness?) to *ovum urinae*—"urine egg." When brought into English, "urine egg" was expressed in English words, *adela eye*—"addle egg."

By 1600, people were using *addle* as an adjective, interpreting its position in the phrase "addle egg" as that of an adjective; in the early 1700s, it was being used as a verb synonymous with *muddle* or *confuse*, and *addled* was being used as an adjective meaning "muddled or confused." And words like *addlepate*, *addlebrain,* and *addlehead* began to surface about the same time.

The major source of addlement here lies in the confusing question (ye gods of punnery, forgive me!) "Which came first, the shittin' or the egg?"

and this is what we put into our mouths?

words of food and drink and taste (and lack thereof)

This section is something of a potpourri of tasty tidbits … well, perhaps a potpourri of tasteless tidbits, which you'll better appreciate when you delve into the origin of the word *potpourri* itself in this chapter.

Please excuse the short introduction; we are skipping the appetizers and going straight to the unappetizers—the entrees themselves. (We will pause later on for some wine with dinner, or in some cases, a lot of wine with dinner, as we also examine words that will have MADD—Mothers Against Drunk Derivations—a little uncomfortable.)

sausage (sort of)

It's a scene worthy of Hannibal Lecter or Jeffrey Dahmer or your favorite cannibal of choice. A human being is slashed open, revealing intestines and other entrails. It's bloody, it's gory, it's … kind of like visiting the meat counter of the grocery store, with its tasty display of neatly packaged sausages.

In the ancient times when this verbal imagery came about, there weren't any grocery stores as we know them, of course. The image may very well have occurred on a field of battle, where someone inclined to odd poetry viewed the insides of the eviscerated, and saw … sausages. (Perhaps the poetry wasn't that odd, in that sausages are meats stuffed into casings—and the original casings were animal intestines.) In Latin, the word for "small intestine" was a diminutive of the word for *sausage*.

We use that word today, by the way, in a couple of forms. The Latin word was *botulus*, which was taken into Old French as *boel*, and into Middle English as *bouel*, what you and I now spell *bowel*. (The other form is *botulism*, the medical term adapted from German, describing not an affliction of the bowel, as one might be prone to guess, but instead a type of food poisoning often associated with ill-prepared processed foods—originally and specifically, sausages.)

Funny, despite the possible connection via shape, there are no pastas named after bowels (see VERMICELLI)—that I've been able to find, at least.

puddiNg

You've likely heard of the Scottish dish (well, especially if you're Scottish) called *haggis*. Haggis is not found on the menu of your local McDonald's (which, despite the name, you'll recall is not a particularly Scottish restaurant). This dish is made by stuffing a sheep's stomach with various minced sheep innards (same sheep, usually), including the heart and lungs and fat and the oats the sheep would likely be putting into its stomach without the help of the cook if the sheep were still alive. Then you boil the stuffed stomach.

After dining on haggis, would you care for some pudding for dessert?

No need. You've already had pudding.

The original puddings were haggis-like concoctions, and ultimately sausage-like concoctions (sausages, after all, before the modern days of food preparation, were minced meats and fats and filler stuffed into animal intestines called *casings* as discussed above). And in fact, the word *pudding* could very well trace back, through Old French *boudin*, to *botulus*—"sausage," in Latin (see also SAUSAGE).

The meaning of *pudding* in the sweet-treat sense arose because preparing early types of pudding involved stuffing ingredients in a bag and steaming or boiling the concoction, and the name stayed with the dessert even after other ways of creating the desserts were employed.

Still, the heck with tapioca pudding and vanilla pudding and chocolate pudding. Let's have a nice, tasty blood pudding, such as one from this recipe found in an untitled medieval cookbook found in the collection of Samuel Pepys (for more, visit www. godecookery.com):

125

To make A podyng of A nox or of A shepe

Take the blode and swyng hit with thy hand and cast a way the lumpys that kyeneth then take sewet of the same and mynse hit small and put in to þe blode also put in plenty of otyn grytts and fyll up thy ropeys with the same and sethe them and after broyle them When they be colde And serue þem forth.

Or in more modern English:

To make a pudding of an ox or of a sheep

Take the blood and hand-beat it, and cast away the lumps that form, then take the suet of the same [that is, of the ox or the sheep] and mince it small and put into the blood; also put in plenty of oaten grits and fill up the intestines with the same and boil them and after broil them. When they be cold, serve them forth.

Hog's pudding is of similar preparation. If you want something a bit fancier, you might try another sort of hog's pudding, this being "fish hog" pudding. A recipe for same appears in another medieval cook book (which you can find if you're hungry enough in *Two Fifteenth-Century Cookery-Books* from Oxford University Press, or in a search on the Web): "Puddyng of purpaysse." (*Purpaysse* being "porpoise," coming from Old French and ultimately from Latin roots *porcus*, "pork," and *piscis*, "fish." In fact, one spelling of *porpoise* in early English was *porpisce*.)

Porpoise pudding: Not coming soon to a Food Network special near you.

humble pie

"Eat humble pie" literally means "eat your words" … *if* your words happen to be "deer entrails."

Umbles or *numbles* (which lost its *n* the way *napple* and *napron* did) are animal entrails, and *umble pie* is pie made of edible (one would hope) innards from such animals as deer and hogs. Resorting to such a repast is not living high on the hog (a phrase that results from being able to afford choice cuts of meat like the ribs and tenderloin that are positioned high near the spine). It's a pretty low meal, and you have to be in humble straits to turn to umble eats.

So, figuratively, eating "humble pie" with its conscious pun on "umble pie," means exercising humility, and eating one's words is one connotation. And clean your plate, young man! You left behind a comma or two.

pie

Those familiar with Asian cooking know that spider rolls (a type of sushi roll actually created in the States) contain not spiders but spider crab, and that Chinese bird's nest soup contains not ... well, not spiders but bird's nests. (We're not talking nests made of twigs and string, but of the hardened saliva of the swiftlet, a type of swallow. We won't dwell on why *swallows* are doing the opposite to create their nests, nor will we dwell on the lameness of a joke based on etymologically unrelated swallows.)

Now, those familiar with Western cooking suspect that pies also contain bird's nests—figuratively, according to one proposed origin of the word *pie*, at least. The word may have come from Latin as opposed to this fowl route. When the first pie-like dishes were created, probably of meat or fish and certainly not of boysenberries, someone may have likened the variegated collection of ingredients to the contents of a magpie's nest. Magpies are known for collecting baubles and such into their nests. And magpies, at the time the word *pie* was used for a baked dish, were known as pies. Thus the suggested connection.

vermicelli

The only time you can use the phrase "baited breath" ("*bated* breath" is correct, of course) is when eating vermicelli pasta.

Vermicelli, so named in Italian because it resembles worms.

Given the fact that there are some 650 types of pasta, it would be hard to avoid naming a pasta after worms. There are just so many nouns, after all.

If vermicelli leaves a bad taste in your mouth, consider ordering the lumaconi pasta. *Lumaconi*: large slugs.

This could be considered the sort of food we informally call *grub* (and have since the 1600s). Though the origin is uncertain, it's generally accepted that *grub* means the insect of the same name—a bit of crunchy metaphor, suggesting that food is to humans what grubs are to birds.

Returning, by the way, to things pasta, some other interesting meanings:

linguine—little tongues

mostaciolli—little mustaches

capellini—hair

orecchiette—little ears

ziti—bridegrooms or boys (The *Merriam-Webster New Book of Word Histories* notes, "This form of pasta is particularly favored at nuptial feasts in the south of Italy; the reason for the name of the pasta may be its phallic shape.")

And *lasagna* deserves a discussion unto itself.

Lasagna

I have yet to find an explanation about the *why* of a certain word borrowing I'll relate in a moment. First, *lasagna* the word came from Italian unchanged. Lasagna is lasagna. The word takes the name of the Roman word for "cooking pot."

But here's where we get to the part where I'm curious and I don't want to know all at the same time. One suggestion is that the word meaning "cooking pot" was *lasania*, in Vulgar Latin. The suggestion continues that *lasania* came from Latin *lasanum*, meaning both "cooking pot" and (well, vulgar indeed) "chamber pot." And that *lasanum* was a borrowing from Greek *lasanon*, "chamber pot." I wonder about the Roman or Romans who decided that a word with such a meaning could be applied to a cooking pot. Perhaps it was a mistake. Perhaps some comic Roman was insulting the results of someone's cooking.

Either way, I suspect I'd rather be eating worms (see VERMICELLI). Or potpourri.

potpourri

The cook who inspired the facetiously fictitious Roman to relate a cooking pot to a chamber pot (see LASAGNA, above) may have inspired some Spaniard to concoct an appetizing name for a type of spicy stew containing all manner of ingredients, including "fruite, flesh, and fish," as described by Richard Hakluyt in 1589. This equally facetiously fictitious Spaniard leaned over to see what was on the menu tonight and said something along the lines of, "That looks very tasty, just like a yummy, bubbling, festering pustule."

The stew's name, of Spanish or Portuguese origin, is *olla podrida*, literally "pot rotten." The slowly boiling stew may have resembled a bubbling pustule, inspiring the name. Or maybe the concoction just plain smelled funny.

The French borrowed the dish's name, translating it as *pot pourri*. (Both *podrida* and *pourri* trace back to Latin for "putrid.") And as *potpourri*, the word came to English, meaning a hodgepodge stew, by the 1600s. By the mid-1700s, the meaning of "flower mixture" had arisen, and by the mid-1800s, the figurative sense of "mixture, medley, pastiche."

How did potpourri drift from stew to flowers? A silly and baseless suggestion: flowers in the stew?

131

COCONUT

If you've seen a coconut in the raw, you've likely noted how the head-sized fruit resembles, well, a head—with a furry face on it. Three holes—two eyes and a small mouth—gaping back at you. The *coco* in *coconut* very likely is a Spanish or Portuguese word with several meanings, including "grinning face or grinning skull," and "goblin, bugbear." *Coco* was what we Americans would call the boogeyman; in his 1706 *A New Spanish and English Dictionary* (well, it was new then), Capt. John Stevens defines the Spanish word: "coco: the word us'd to fright children, as we say the Bulbeggar."

So why are we using pumpkins and not coconuts as Halloween decorations?

BROKER

Early versions of the three-martini lunch gave us a word for a type of businessperson that engages in three-martini lunches.

In the Anglo-French the word originated from, a *broker* was one who "broached" the cask of wine and sold the wine itself. A broker was a tapster.

By extension, a broker became by 1400 anyone who bought something to resell, or a dealer of secondhand goods, or one who made purchases for other people—the as-of-yet-uneliminated middleman. This generalized meaning became for a time tainted with disdain for such work. One obsolete meaning of *broker* was "pimp" (with *brokeress* meaning "madam").

These days on Wall Street, after a hard day at work, you'll likely see brokers stopping in at the local watering hole to patronize their brokers.

BRIðaL

A toast to the bride!

At the wedding, certainly. At the bridal shower, almost certainly. At the bridal shop? Now, isn't all this toasting getting a little carried away? And another toast to the bride! And, hell, let's party!

Bridal began life as a noun—the adjective meaning "related to brides or weddings" staggered in later. And I say "staggered in" because originally a bridal was a "bride-ale."

Ale as in the alcoholic beverage, though a later meaning of *ale* was "feast or celebration"—where, of course, there was a lot of ale sloshing around. (The use is similar to calling a more sedate gathering with a more sedate beverage of choice a *tea*.) The wedding feast, therefore, was a bride-ale.

And another toast to the bride!

Various sorts of ales were held in days gone by. They were celebrations and fundraisers, like the scot-ale (*scot* as in "payment"). There were church-ales and Mary-ales and clerk-ales (held to benefit parish clerks). Related to funerals, soul-ales and dirge-ales. There were help-ales, thrown for people who helped accomplish a big job, like mowing the hay (think a bigger version of buying beer and pizza for friends who help you move). There were lamb-ales and Midsummer-ales. In 1570, William Kethe wrote, "The multitude call Church-ale Sunday their revelyng day, which day is spent in bulbeatings, bearbeating, … dicying, … and drunkenness."

Apparently, the bride-ale had much revelying, as well. In 1587, William Harrison referred to "the heathenish rioting at bride-ales" in *The Description of England*.

By 1300, an alternate spelling was in use: *bridal*, the meaning of which was extended from wedding feast to the wedding and all related festivities and proceedings. By the 1700s, adjective use had arrived (as in "bridal shop"), influenced by other common adjectives ending in -al (e.g., *fatal*, *archival*, *mortal*). Kind of unguilt by association.

But until the feast deteriorates into a late evening of weak adjectives … A toasht to da bride!

snack

Next time you head to the kitchen to get a snack, beware the dog.

It might make a snack out of you—by taking a snack *at* you.

A snap of the jaws is the snack, or the bite that results from a snap of the jaws, usually applied to dogs. The word was in use as a verb by the 1300s and as a noun by the early 1400s. By the late 1600s, *snack* came to mean a portion, a bit—or a small amount of liquor (a mouthful, perhaps?). By the mid-1700s, it was a small amount of food, or a meal composed of a small amount of food—what you're seeking from the fridge or the cupboard.

But watch the dog, and your backside. If the dog snacks at you, you can snack back in kind. Not by biting the dog and riling up the newspaper reporters, but by scolding the attacking mutt. Because a snack could also be a rebuke or a sharp remark. "'Don't snack me!' he snacked. 'I must snack!'"

The word *snap* has an almost identical history—*snack* is likely from Middle Dutch or Low German, and *snap* is almost assuredly so. And *snap* also has the meanings of "bite at" or "speak sharply." But not the "bit of consumables" part, right?

Depends on what you're getting out of the refrigerator. *Snappen* ("to seize") eventually led to English *snap*, but it also led to *snaps* ("mouthful"), which led to German *schnapps*, which we borrowed into English by the early 1800s.

"Don't snap at me!" he snapped. "I must have schnapps!"

BALDERDASH

With a dash of beer and a dash of wine and a dash of balder, you have a delectable drink: the balderdash.

That very well sounds like the type of nonsense that the exclamation *balderdash!* describes, but there's more than a drop of truth to that odd concoction. The "dash of balder" is thrown in as wordplay, but one early meaning of *balderdash* was a mixture of liquids, such as combination wine and beer. Or—who thinks this stuff up?—beer and buttermilk. This nonsensical liquid hodgepodge was extended to verbal nonsensical hodgepodge, and the bombastic nonsense itself.

Quaff enough of those odd mixtures (especially that buttermilk-beer soup) and you'll soon be spewing balderdash both figuratively and literally.

YEN

Ever crave something, but you don't know what? Have a yen for something?

If you have a yen, you probably don't have a clue about what that yen is for—or at least what it used to be for. *Yen* looks innocent enough, looking similar to *yearn* as it does. *Yearn*, however, reaches all the way back to Old English. *Yen* reaches back all the way to the last half of the nineteenth century.

The word comes from Chinese, and not long after the turn of the century *yen* began to take its modern meaning. But a yen originally was a craving, and a pretty deep craving at that—for opium.

So next time you have a yen for something but can't figure out what … might I suggest potato chips?

WINGDING

A wingding is an informal reference to a wild party, a big to-do, a hullabaloo, a festive and intense celebration. It's easy to design a guest list for a wingding. Just invite all the folks with yens (see above)—invite all the drug addicts you know.

The present slang sense of *wingding* arose by the late 1940s, but the word arose by 1927 as an origin-unknown slang word for a physical fit or seizure. Specific to the context of this book is that it often described a *false* seizure. Some drug addicts faked spasms, hoping for attention from medical professionals—and the narcotics that the medical professionals might use to calm them. The spasm was a wingding.

Getting what they wanted apparently put them in a party mood.

tobacconist

Today, you'll find a tobacconist behind the counter selling tobacco.

Before the mid-1600s, you'd find the tobacconist in front of the counter, buying it. And probably suffering from some cravings while doing so.

First use of the word *tobacconist* was somewhat along the analogy of the noun *alcoholic*. A tobacconist was a heavy user, perhaps one addicted.

It's safe to surmise that many of the tobacconists in the current meaning of the word are tobacconists in the initial meaning, given the fact that tobacco shops do not likely have nonsmoking sections.

petunia

Speaking of nonsmoking sections, best not try to grow petunias there. Not that a petunia is anything someone would try to smoke. Well, maybe in the sixties; I won't rule out the possibility of that sort of herbal experimentation during that free-form time period.

Yet, the concept isn't as drug-whacked as it might first sound, as there is indeed a certain type of tobacco smoldering in the very core of the word *petunia*.

Petun is a now-rare word from the mid-1500s (from French and ultimately from native North American languages) meaning "tobacco plant."

Petunias are related to tobacco plants not only through the science of etymology, but also the science of botany—petunias are biologically related to tobacco plants.

symposium

"Honey! I'm off to the symposium!"

All business and learning, that. Soaking up wisdom, drinking in knowledge.

Well, drinking anyway.

Originally, a symposium was likely to be held in the presence of your broker (see above). There could be some learning going on, as symposia were indeed often held for conversation and, as the *Oxford English Dictionary* phrases it, "intellectual entertainment" such as riddles, jokes, and poetry. But the core of the symposium, and the core of the word *symposium*, was drinking. A symposium was a gathering for drinking. The word, brought in from Latin by the late 1500s, traces back to a Greek word meaning "drinking companion"—*sumpotes*, according to John Ayto's *Dictionary of Word Origins*.

The modern sense of a formal gathering to discuss a particular topic surfaces by the late 1700s—and now that I've shared that bit of knowledge in this simple little symposium, it's time to join my sumpotes for a beer.

i am not an animal!
i am an etymologyist!

words of the birds and the beasts

Animals are by technical definition living things that move. Insects, amoebas, orangutans. Words are, in a sense, themselves animals. They are figuratively living things. They feed off one another, and they grow. And as we've seen, they move about.

Some words are even born of animals. At their origins are creatures of the Earth, though we no longer hear them bark or moo.

Here, then, is a petting zoo of words that, true to their animal origins, have moved from **one** meaning to another. We start with, appropriately enough, an animal word that describes words.

jargon

Go to a convention of any type of specialized professionals—doctors, engineers, etymologists—and try to jot down what they're saying. You'll catch a few English words tossed in here and there, maybe a few English syllables detached from real words and reattached to some mumblings and euphemisms and inside jokes. But overall, you might as well be sitting near a telephone wire with row upon row of perched crows and trying to transliterate their twittering.

The crows and the specialists are actually displaying the same thing: *jargon.*

Twittering birds, twittering specialists. The birds were first.

The word could also describe vocal sounds reminiscent of twittering sounds, and eventually came to mean gibberish or babble or an instance of something beyond understanding. The sense of a lingo or body of specialized terminology came about in the mid-1600s. All that is what etymologists sometimes call "transference of meaning." Or so a little bird told me. A flock of twittering little birds, actually.

It's likely that these specialists sharing a jargon are gregarious—they like to group together, converse, share ideas. But once again, the birds were first.

The birds and the bees and the buffalo and the wolves—in technical zoological language, these creatures group together in communities, flocks, or herds. *Gregarious* was borrowed from Latin by the mid-1600s to describe animal behavior and was applied figuratively to people by the late 1700s. The ultimate root in Latin was *grex*, "flock, herd." And when we congregate, we herd ourselves. When we aggregate, we herd something else. When we segregate, we split up the herd. When we do something egregious, we do something beyond the herd.

So the first social animals were *truly* animals.

cockpit

Let's hope the pilots in the cockpit of your airliner or the drivers in the cockpits of NASCAR cars aren't of a mind to play chicken—the test of manhood where two combatants aim directly for each other until one of them "chickens out."

Though, in the very first cockpits, that's exactly what they did. Well, not pilots or drivers. But actual chickens. Male chickens. Cocks.

Cockpits (from the 1500s) were exactly what the word implies: pits where cockfights were held. Roosters with spiked spurs tearing each other apart. The word was used figuratively to describe any theater of combat by the early 1600s, and then by the early 1900s to the places (in airplanes) where combatants sat. Bombs, unlike spurs, making more than feathers fly.

(As a side note, the declaration "I'm game," meaning "I'm willing" or "I'm able," comes from the spirit and pluck of one of those fighting cocks—the gamecock.)

muscle

Though mice are not generally known for their muscles, muscles are somewhat known for their mice. Etymologically speaking, that is.

We've all heard the cliché "rippling muscles," and indeed in certain types of muscular action we can see movement underneath the skin. There's an earthy poetry in noticing, in early observations of the body, that these ripples look a little like a mouse scooting around beneath the skin. Thus, the cause of the ripples was referred to as a "little mouse"—in Latin, a *musculus*, the diminutive form of *mus*, or "mouse." That meaning was well in place in Latin by the time it was adapted into Late Middle English.

(Kind of makes your skin crawl, doesn't it?)

So, in answering the question, "Are you a man or a mouse?" our friends the bodybuilders might actually opt for the latter.

god forbid

God forbid that we learn one meaning of "God forbid."

We use the phrase in asking providence to prevent disaster or hardship. Lose your job? God forbid! Your lover dumps you? God forbid! A tornado lands? God forbid!

But in the early 1900s the request was re-geared as rhyming slang, with a specific hardship in mind. "Please, no more mouths to feed! No more children!"

God forbid rhymes with *kid*, and one use of the phrase was not as a sentence but as a noun phrase. Your *kids* were your *God forbids*.

porcelain

Compliment an etymologically aware lady about her porcelain skin and she's likely to call you a pig, or more eloquently a pig's dick, just to return the favor.

Porcelain takes its name from *porcellana*, an Italian word for "cowrie shell." (An aside: there is no "cow" in *cowrie*, so we aren't on a barnyard theme here. Yet.) The smooth surface of the ceramic, brought back to Italy from China by Marco Polo, reminded the Italians of the surface of the cowrie. All well and good.

But how did *porcellana*, ultimately tracing back to Latin *porcus* ("pig," as in our word *pork*), become associated with cowrie shells?

Though not a certainty, some etymologists hold to or do not discount the theory that the word comes from the fact that shell resembles a sow's vulva (another theory, stated less regularly, is that the connection may be between the ridges along the shell and the ridge of a pig's back). Should the cowrie-vulva etymology be true, one must wonder what kind of worldly experience someone had in order to be familiar enough with both ocean biology and domestic-animal anatomy to be able to make such a visual comparison.

Ruminate

Let's ruminate on cows chewing their cud.

In other words, ruminate on rumination.

The first stomach of a ruminant animal (that is, an animal that chews its cud) is a *rumen*. *Rumen* is a Latin word that led to Latin *ruminari*, which in turn led to the English word *ruminate* by the early 1500s. A cud, by the way, is partially digested food that is returned from the first stomach to the animal's mouth for further chewing.

So chew that image over in your mind and chew it again—ruminate it.

If you're reading this in the bookstore, and have just shooed away a clerk (or are about to) by saying, "Just browsing," keep in mind that browsing in its original literal sense was (as for the cow mentioned in the item above) grazing on grasses or on the leaves of bushes and trees—something I might have to do if you continue figuratively browsing. Hey—just a hint! (While you're browsing and ruminating, go buy *Eats, Shoots & Leaves* by Lynn Truss, too.)

cowslip

Such a pretty flower, the cowslip. And such a poetic name, originating from "cow's lip" (somewhat like the way "day's eye" became *daisy*). Look at the flower carefully, and you can see those mooing lips and …

Well, that etymology is bullshit.

And the *cowslip* itself is bullshit. At least the word is.

There's no *lip* in *cowslip*. There is, instead, the Old English *slyppe*. A cowslip is a *cu-slyppe*. *Cu* is "cow," *slyppe* is "dung or slime or slobber." Early flower-namers noted that the cowslip grows where there's a lot of natural fertilizer.

Such a pretty flower, the cowdung.

I spent some youthful years on a dairy farm, by the by. We had various terms for the large splatted droppings that dotted the pastures. One was *cow-pie* and another was *cow-chip*, which has such appropriate rhyme and resonance with *cowslip*.

BELLWETHER

Unlike the belfry, there have always been bells associated with the bellwether. Or at least one bell. The bellwether likely wishes there were more "bells" involved.

Figuratively, a *bellwether* is an "indicator of trends." Where the bellwether goes, the marketplace (for instance) follows. The bellwether shows us which way the wind is going to blow, even though the word has nothing to do with weather.

Literally, a *bellwether* is "the lead sheep." He has been adorned with a bell that keeps the attention of the other sheep. Wherever the bellwether goes, the sheep follow. Like sheep.

Now a *wether* by itself does not, as mentioned before, have "bells" in the euphemistic sense. A *wether* is a castrated sheep. The bellwether's only bell is artificial.

Butterfly

Butterflies, fluttering and floating daintily from one part of the meadow to another, from one proposed etymology to another, crapping all over the place, stealing your dairy goods.

Didn't realize that butterflies were such rascals, did you?

No one's quite sure about the origin of the word *butterfly*, but two suggested origins are popular.

The first is that the word results from the notion that butterflies are attracted to butter—and in folklore the insects were actually witches or fairies come to steal your butter. Now, to modern eyes there's no apparent logic to most such notions (knock on wood to scare away the little demons that live within?), but if I were a witch or a fairy with magical power sufficient enough to turn myself into an insect, I'd likely find a more efficient way to go dairy shoplifting. (On the other hand, there's a German word for "butterfly" that means "milk thief": *Milchdieb*. Another German word for "butterfly," *Schmetterling*, comes from a root meaning "cream.")

The second proposal suggests that *butter* refers to the color of the insect's excrement. Now, quickly reviewing a mental zoo, I can't come up with another example of an animal named for the color of its excrement. People tend to notice other things about animals first. Will they fetch? Are they tasty? Are they about to pounce on you with sharp claws and pointy teeth and take you home to the cubs for supper? And, as long as we're speculating on the logic of animal observations, who is aware that insects, of all things, have excrement in the first place? Okay, there's the honey thing (but even there it's more purging than excrement), and usually our concern about the topic of animal excrement involves walking carefully on urban sidewalks and in pastures (see also COWSLIP) and cursing low-flying birds when returning to a car that's been parked outside all day (see also MISTLETOE). Insect excrement seems an unlikely topic of such major concern that an entire class of insect is named for it. (On another other hand, there's a Dutch word for butterfly, *boterschijte*, which means "butter" ... well, you can figure it out, and it's not "milk thief.")

Likely, the color of butter is indeed at the core of the word's origin, but more likely candidates are the buttery or, for that matter, creamy wing color of certain butterflies, or a poetic nod to the color of the plants the b-flies are visiting.

Ultimately, the fanciful but probably untrue witch and crap etymologies should simply be allowed to spooneristically flutter by.

Larva, caterpillar

If we subscribe to the theory that *butterfly* (see above) is somehow related to supernatural beings taking the form of beautiful insects in order to steal dairy commodities, we find an interesting connection to one stage of the butterfly's life.

Caterpillars are soft and cuddly and cute and all that, so we tend not to think of them by their more technical designation. Caterpillars are butterfly larvae.

And larvae are demons in disguise.

You can infer the Latin origin in *larva* in the construction of its plural as demonstrated above. In Latin, *larva* had two meanings: "devil or hobgoblin" and "mask." English adopted the devilish meaning by the mid-1600s. By the mid-1700s the mask meaning was applied to creatures in their larval stage because they were, at that stage of development, masking their eventual form.

The interesting and circumstantial connections continue. *Caterpillar* arises from a French word meaning "hairy cat." Martha Barnette, in *Dog Days and Dandelions*, points out that "In Switzerland, a caterpillar is sometimes called a *Teufelskatz*—or 'devil's cat.'" (Does that sound, um, *familiar*?) So is this devil really ultimately seeking to engage in buttery thievery? As Barnette continues, "The word *caterpillar*'s final form may have been influenced by the obsolete English word *piller*, which means 'robber, plunderer, or thief,' and a relative of *pillage*."

Circumstantial evidence implicating the butterfly as otherworldly thief, but I rest my case.

ᛞogged

A dogged person is determined and persistent, perhaps to the point of being obstinate. Looking at the first syllable, it's easy to allow an image of a *physical* dog to come to mind, fetching a stick but refusing to let go when you try to take the stick.

The image of a physical dog is misleading, because—well, it's not misleading at all. The *dog* in *dogged* is indeed a dog. In fact, *dogged* was first used as an adjective synonymous with both our contemporary words *doglike* and *canine*.

By the early 1300s, the word was applied to people pejoratively. If you were dogged, you had doglike traits—the bad ones. You cur!

For a time, the pejoration intensified: A dogged person had the traits of particularly bad dogs (and bad people too)—maliciousness, spite, cruelty. Then it in turn softened a bit, so that a dogged person was surly and sullen. Then sullenly stubborn. And now just stubborn, with positive connotations. A dogged effort is tireless. A dogged person does not give up. He's got that stick in his teeth and won't let go. A good thing, because in etymological times past, that dogged person just might bite you.

puce

Do you feel well-dressed wearing puce? Puce is a dark color that would indeed befit the most sartorial, the ostentatious, the rich, the famed, and the famous. In fact, puce would certainly suit the clothing of those used to performing before audiences—say, opera singers, actresses and, oh, the stars of the flea circus. Yes, the flea-circus performer is naturally well costumed, decked out as it is in natural puce. *Puce*, which came to English by the late 1700s, ultimately comes from Old French *couleur puce*, or, literally, "flea color."

Gives a whole new potential taste to puce lipstick, doesn't it? (And that thought makes the pronunciation of *puce* suddenly seem appropriate.)

Nitpick

Each. Little. Detail.

Every. Tiny. Flaw.

The nitpicker will find them. Each. And. Every. One.

Like the excessive, tiny periods in the above "sentences." They don't belong. Get rid of them. Take a fine-tooth comb to those sentences.

This is an appropriate action for the nitpicker—using the fine-tooth comb, that is. Such an instrument can help you find those things that are about the size of a punctuation period (I assume, having never encountered one personally that I know of): the nit.

A nit is a louse egg.

To pick nits is to inspect (usually human) hair for the eggs of lice. (The louse egg may also be the *nit* in *nitwit*.) And *nitpicker*—the figurative flaw-finder—arises out of twentieth-century military slang (along with *flyspecker*, and we all know what those flyspecks are, don't we?).

misceLLaneous
disguises and surprises

words that start and end
with double-ewwww!

It is now time for a potpourri of—well, maybe not, especially if you consult the entry for potpourri.

Then perhaps it is now time for a medley of—well, let's back off that one, too (see page 12 for an etymologist's attack on *medley* and vice versa).

Miscellany. That is a purposeful word with no hidden meanings. *Miscellany* means "miscellany" no matter how far back you trace its ancestry.

Congratulations, *miscellany*. You've passed the background check.

Have you had a moment to look up *potpourri*, by the way? Given the nature of the entries below, and given *miscellany*'s innocence, let's go ahead and more appropriately introduce the following uncategorizable thoughts and musings on words with unseemly or surprising disguises as a potpourri.

We begin not with a word that starts with double-ewww! but with a simple W. We begin with with (which is not a slip of the keyboard, as you'll see).

WITH

"Are you with me or against me?"

"Yes."

This conversation does not seem improbable or humorous if you consider that *with* first connoted (among other obsolete senses) "against." Consider the following phrases:

- fight against
- compete against
- struggle against

In each of those examples, insert *with* to replace *against* (I'd instruct you to replace *against* with *with*, but that sounds a little odd). *Fight with, compete with, struggle with*—you likely see the sense of "against" more clearly now. Consider also *withstand* and *withhold*.

So, "Are you with me or against me?" translated to "Are you against me or against me?" makes yes a sensible answer.

pREposteRous (OR, pREposteRous!)

We're about to take a bit of a wandering etymological journey, so hop on the cart while I hitch it up in front of the horse.

The cart before the horse? That's a preposterous concept.

Cart-then-horse is a concept of something in front that should be behind. The posterior precedes. *Prepost-erous!*

In a very early sense, *preposterous* (from Latin, of course) meant what we in less formal terms might call *ass-backwards* (or even, using the delightfully ass-backwards word, *bass-ackwards*). From that sense arose our modern sense of "absurd" (a sense it also held in Latin), because why would anyone put that damn cart before the horse?

Maybe cart-then-horse was a fundamental decision. Or a decision involving fundament. Who wants to sit behind the horse's fundament? A *fundament* was originally the foundation of a building or other structure (and *fundamental* was originally "related to the foundation of a building or other structure") but very early on was also "the behind, the arse, the buttocks." ("Anus," as well.)

The croupier might be perfectly happy to sit if not behind the horse's fundament, then at least on it. How did gambling get into this picture? Certainly we aren't racing our cart-then-horse in some whacked-out version of harness racing. Besides, we see croupiers at craps tables and roulette wheels. (There might be wheels and craps involved with all this horse talk, but both are quite beside the point for the moment.)

In English, a *croupier* was first "a gamester's second" before the word came to mean the person who takes away all your money and chips at the game table (both meanings from the 1700s). The word, with its gaming meanings, came from the French, where it was created by analogy with the person who rides a horse behind the primary rider on the croup—*croup* meaning "horse's hindquarters, behind," etc.—that is, who rides the horse behind the saddle.

At least we're not talking about putting the cart on the horse, behind the saddle. Now that would truly be preposterous!

pReposteROUS, pARt ii

Preposterous is, in its original sense, something of a preposterous word. It is created from Latin roots: *pre-* (before) and *post-* (after). The word itself is therefore bass-ackwards by its syllables being in illogically logical order. That is to say, shouldn't the word really be *postpreperous* or *posterpreous*, with the "after" out front?

peNtHOUSe

You've certainly heard the cliché "from the penthouse to the outhouse," meaning to tumble from the top down to the depths, to go from living high and luxuriantly to landing in the crapper.

Through the wonders of ancient etymology, you can go from penthouse to outhouse without even moving.

No, we're not talking about some beam-me-up-Scotty sort of science fiction mechanism that transports you from one place to another. With the original meanings of both *penthouse* and *outhouse*, when you are in one you are automatically in the other. They both meant the same thing.

They went their separate ways, of course. *Penthouse* went up; *outhouse* burrowed a few feet down. But both originally meant a building separate from the main building. Recorded first in the 1300s, an *outhouse* was a structure outside the main structure—for instance, a barn or a shed. It could be attached or detached. *Outhouse* began taking its specific sense as outdoor privy by the early 1800s, in the States. The word's construction, like the building itself, was simple. It was a house that was out.

Penthouse had arrived in English by 1400. It, too, meant a type of outhouse, though one attached to the main building. The word derives ultimately from a French verb meaning "to append." By the late 1800s, the penthouse was still attached but positioned up top instead of aside. Construction of the word *penthouse*, much like the modern-day penthouse itself, was considerably more complex than that of *outhouse*. The word came to English as *pentiz* or a variation thereof. The *Oxford English Dictionary* notes more than forty spelling variants before it was altered to look more like the word we use today. Folk etymology converted the second syllable to one more familiar in English, and one true to what it described: *house*.

So *outhouse* had less, um, aromatic roots, while its near synonym was far earthier than it is today.

suggestion

Dr. Faustus was merely taking a suggestion when he sold his soul to the devil.

Suggestion, by the mid 1300s, was "enticement or prodding to evil," especially when conducted by the dark one (the *original* dark one, though in this context "Come to the Dark Side, Luke" is a suggestion, as well). And to *suggest*, the verb form in use by the early 1500s, was "to propose something evil." This was taking the power of suggestion to a whole new level—or actually, a whole *old* level. General uses soon followed, of course, and for *suggestion* the sense of evil enticement had died out by the mid-1600s.

Ironically, we see weak echoes of the original sense of *suggestion* and *suggest* in the word *suggestive*, which by the late 1800s was used to describe something that implies if not evil, then at least a little naughtiness. This sense, considered a euphemism, does not seem to rise directly from the original meaning of *suggestion*.

But for the potential Dr. Faustuses of the world, in today's medical workplace (and most workplaces), the suggestion box is a place to request the end and not the instigation of sexual harassment.

sophisticated

Call someone sophisticated today, and you praise that person as cultured, refined. Call some*thing* sophisticated today, and you praise it as well-designed, state-of-the-art, complex, and useful. And so in a broad sense, the word *sophisticated* has become unsophisticated.

To *sophisticate* something was "to adulterate it, mix it with something inferior." It was made more complex, robbed of simplicity. It was not genuine. Like the word *sophisticated*. It has been mixed with something inferior—today's positive meanings, robbing us of an ancient word associated with sophistry, the art of false argument.

Luxury

Giorgio Armani is quoted as saying, "I'll tell you something: Luxury disgusts me." Armani apparently knows his etymology.

Luxury, coming through Old French from Latin, meaning "enjoying or indulging in abundance," with negative connotations, meant "lechery" and "lust" when it came to English by the 1300s. Says Thersites in Shakespeare's *Troilus and Cressida*: "How the devil Luxury, with his fat rump and potato-finger, tickles these together! Fry, lechery, fry!"

Other hints of wantonness are associated, as in Chaucer's "Pardoner's Tale":

> Singers with harpes, baudes, waferers,
> Which be the very devil's officers,
> To kindle and blow the fire of lechery,
> That is annexed unto gluttony.
> The Holy Writ take I to my witness,
> That luxury is in wine and drunkenness.

Senses of less distasteful abundances and pleasures started by the early 1600s. Still, etymologically, when you dream of being in the lap of luxury, you'd better be careful about just whose lap is involved.

paraphernalia

Paraphernalia—accessories, the miscellaneous, the not-so-important stuff.

And something of a word helping to form a sexist statement.

Under old British common law, when a man and woman married, ownership of the wife's personal property was transferred to the husband. But the wife was "granted" free use of some of the items—clothing, jewels, toiletries, and other items not so important to husbands (unless they were cross-dressers, I suppose)—and after the husband died, she was allowed to keep these items. Such allowances were *paraphernalia bona*, based on Roman law, and the phrase traces back to roots meaning "apart from the dowry." More general uses of *paraphernalia* were cropping up by the 1700s, though the law the word is based on was in place until the late 1800s. Under *paraphernalia bona*, the husband owns the dowry (and everything else, it seems), but at least the wife gets to use some of what she used to own.

success

I leave the main section of *Unfortunate English* with this thought: Everything you do is successful. Everything.

This is not some sort of self-help mantra. This is not some sort of lie for puffing up résumés or personal ads. This is a simple statement of fact.

Everything you do has an outcome. And *success* in the 1500s originally meant "outcome"—that which succeeds or follows. For example, we might refer to someone being caught for burglary and the *succeeding* trial and conviction. Those succeeding events are the success—the outcome, the upshot—of being caught. Hardly the kind of success the burglar was seeking, and *success* in its earliest uses referred to outcomes both good and bad. The conviction was, for the burglar, "ill success," and for the prosecutor, "good success." Also in the 1500s the narrowed meaning of the word came into play, and over time, it took over. (On the other hand, *succeed* retains both meanings, as in—to use our hypothetical burglary conviction—a succeeding or winning attorney in the succeeding or resulting trial. And the verb came first, so we should note that *success* succeeded *succeed*.)

after words

parting thoughts

I leave you, O dedicated and likely disgusted reader, with just two thoughts, two words. The first, a word of parting to discuss a thought of parting.

goodbye

Do atheists ever bid anyone *goodbye*—the contraction of "God be with you?"

Perhaps a better choice of a parting word would be *adieu*—except that if you look closely at it, you can see the roots of *deity* in *adieu*, and in fact it means the same thing as *goodbye*. Nor would a phrase like "Vaya con Dios"—"travel with God," or, more commonly, *adios*, with its reference to the deity as obvious as is it in *adieu*. Safer, perhaps, to say *ciao*—though it has the potentially offensive meaning of "I am your slave." A different political incorrectness not to be pondered for long.

CURMUDGEON

A *curmudgeon* is kind of a grouchy fellow—cynical, crusty, cantankerous—the kind who writes books of unseemly word histories. Early curmudgeons were mean and moneygrubbing; the word has softened since its earliest recorded appearance in the 1570s.

No one knows how *curmudgeon* originated. Despite what Dr. Johnson wrote in 1755's *A Dictionary of the English Language*, and despite what you might think of the writer of books of unseemly word histories, the word does *not* come from a translation of two French words meaning "evil heart."

Just thought you'd like to know.

seLecteÐ
BiBLiogRapHy

Following is a portion of the works I consulted in putting *Unfortunate English* together. Not all of them, of course, as these are selected (you think I was kidding in the title?).

I begin with my favorite and cherished history of and paean to English. It is a general history, but to ignore it would rob you of the ultimate purpose of this book and of so many other wonderful books about word histories: to illuminate the wondrous and fascinating and incredibly rich transformation and adaptation of the gorgeous English language.

Our Marvelous Native Tongue, Robert Claiborne (Three Rivers Press, 1987). Out of print but as of this writing still available for purchase on the Web and, I'm certain, elsewhere. Find this book. Read this book. Revel in this book. Claiborne is informative, articulate, and entertaining. I was honored to work with the gentleman, by the way, on a single project: He wrote an article entitled "Defending the Indefensible" for me when I was editor of *Writer's Digest* magazine. I have been enriched by his wit and scholarship and gentlemanly nature, and

I mourn his passing. Other Claiborne titles: *Loose Cannons, Red Herrings, and Other Lost Metaphors* (W.W. Norton & Company, 2001) and *The Roots of English*, (Crown, 1989). *Roots* is for the hard-core; it's a dictionary of Indo-European roots of English (though those roots fed many other languages, as well).

Other works consulted:

- *Ballyhoo, Buckaroo, and Spuds: Ingenious Tales of Words and Their Origins*, by Michael Quinion, (Smithsonian Books, 2004).

- *The Barnhart Concise Dictionary of Etymology*, by Robert K. Barnhart (HarperResource, 1995).

- *A Browser's Dictionary and Native's Guide to the Unknown American Language*, by John Ciardi (Harper & Row, 1980), and *A Second Browser's Dictionary and Native's Guide to the Unknown American Language*, by John Ciardi (Harper & Row, 1983).

- *Devious Derivations: Popular Misconceptions—and More Than 1,000 True Origins of Common Words and Phrases*, by Hugh Rawson (Crown, 1994).

- *Dictionary of Word Origins: The Histories of More Than 8,000 English-Language Words*, by John Ayto (Arcade Publishing, 1993).

- *Dog Days and Dandelions: A Lively Guide to the Animal Meanings Behind Everyday Words*, by Martha Barnette (St. Martin's Press, 2003).

- *An Etymological Dictionary of Modern English*, vols. I and II, by Ernest Weekley (Dover Publications, 1967), reprint of 1921 edition.

- *A History of English in Its Own Words*, by Craig M. Carver (HarperCollins, 1991).

- *The Merriam-Webster New Book of Word Histories* (Merriam-Webster, 1991).

- *Morris Dictionary of Word and Phrase Origins*, second ed., by William and Mary Morris (HarperCollins, 1988).

- *The New Shorter Oxford English Dictionary on Historical Principles*, vols. I and II, edited by Lesley Brown (Clarendon Press, 1993).

- *NTC's Dictionary of Changes in Meanings*, by Adrian Room (National Textbook Co., 1991).

- *Word Histories and Mysteries: From Abracadabra to Zeus*, by the editors of the American Heritage Dictionaries (Houghton Mifflin Company, 2004).

- *Word Myths: Debunking Linguistic Urban Legends*, by David Wilton, Oxford University Press, New York (2004).

web sites

- **www.bartleby.com**, which includes *The American Heritage Dictionary of the English Language*

- **www.dictionary.com** and **www.thesaurus.com**

- **www.etymonline.com**

- **www.funwords.com**, Martha Barnette's Web site

- The Mavens' Word of the Day, **www.random house.com/wotd/index.pperl?action=dly_ _alph_ arc&fn=word**

- **www.oed.com**, the *Oxford English Dictionary* online

- **www.verbivore.com**, Richard Lederer's Web site

- **www.word-detective.com**, operated by Evan Morris

- **www.wordorigins.org**, from David Wilton includes a lively discussion forum

- **www.worldwidewords.org**, Michael Quinion's Web site

index

179

about
the author

Bill Brohaugh is the author of *Write Tight*, about concision in writing (ISI Books), and *The Grill of Victory*, profiling the competition barbecue circuit (Emmis Books). For Writer's Digest Books, he is the author or editor of *Professional Etiquette for Writers*, *English Through the Ages* and *Just Open a Vein*. He has written several hundred published or produced magazine articles and short radio pieces. He can spell "eclectic."

For updates and additional grumblings, visit www. UnfortunateEnglish.com.